HAUNTED PORTAGE, WISCONSIN

HAUNTED PORTAGE, WISCONSIN

SHELLEY MORDINI AND SHARON HART ADDY

Haunted America

Published by Haunted America
A division of The History Press
An imprint of Arcadia Publishing
Charleston, SC
www.historypress.com

Front cover: Raulf Hotel. *Wikimedia Commons*.

First published 2025

Manufactured in the United States

ISBN 9781467156509

Library of Congress Control Number: 2025937574

This book is dedicated to all the moms and dads, aunts and uncles, brothers and sisters who have gone before and come back in mystical ways, adding mystery to lives in Portage and everywhere.

CONTENTS

ACKNOWLEDGEMENTS

During our yearlong research into hauntings and sightings in the Portage area, we met many folks who offered information, encouragement and personal stories. We're especially thankful for the assistance of the following people:

- Judy and Dave Eulberg
- Gwen Herrewig and Justin Strawther
- Fred Galley of The Galley Studio
- Chris Okan of S.I.G.H.T (Spirit Investigating Ghost Hunting Twins)
- Shad Thorston of the Wisconsin Paranormal Society
- Keith Bylewski of Wisconsin Investigating the Paranormal
- John Lewis Peruzzi Jr., director of Development for Habitat for Humanity of Wisconsin River Area
- The staff of Museum at the Portage
- The staff of the Portage Public Library, with special thanks to Patti Fitcher
- The staffs of the Baraboo Public Library and Wisconsin's South Central Library System
- Portage Chamber of Commerce, with special thanks to Brad Conrad, marketing and event coordinator, and Marianne Hansen, president and CEO

- The Wisconsin DAR, with special thanks to Sandra Snow, state regent, and Cindy McLaughlin, state curator, at Fort Winnebago and the Surgeon's Quarters
- The staff at the Indian Agency House
- And the many wonderful people we met as we visited stores, lunched at local restaurants and gathered stories in person and by phone.

INTRODUCTION

It wasn't our idea to write this book. When *Haunted Baraboo* authors Gwen Herrewig and Shelley Mordini visited the Portage Library to do a presentation about their book, two things impressed them. First was the large group that showed up for a library event, and second, the number of people who said, "Portage needs a book like that." The idea for *Haunted Portage* was born.

However, in 2023, life changed for Gwen. She wouldn't be able to help gather information and write *Haunted Portage*. Sharon Addy stepped in to take her place.

We, Shelley and Sharon, began in July 2023 by contacting the Portage Library and asking who we should talk to. The lady we spoke to suggested we contact Judy Eulberg, a volunteer at the Museum at the Portage. We arranged to meet her at Neil's Wine and Bourbon House and discuss the project over lunch.

Before lunch, we visited the Indian Agency House. Viewing the exhibits and touring the house, as well as talking to the well-informed curator, gave us the basis of information we needed for that segment of Portage's early history, but we left knowing we needed to learn a great deal more.

Judy met us, as arranged, for lunch at Neil's, which was a marvelous idea. The food was good, the atmosphere relaxing and the company excellent. Judy proved to be a knowledgeable woman. She regaled us with wonderful stories of Portage and whet our appetite for more. Judy doesn't believe in ghosts, but she does believe in Portage and supports it wholeheartedly. Her tantalizing tidbits about local history had us eager to research. We were looking forward to meeting people and hearing what they had to say. As time went on, we discovered that—like the Yellow Brick Road in *The Wizard of Oz*—all roads led to Judy. Over and over, we were told to "talk to Judy."

We'd told Judy we would need pictures for the book. She said we should get in touch with Fred Galley. We called his studio and left a message. When we didn't get a response, we sent an email. Then we waited. And we waited. We had no idea that at the end of summer, he'd be one of the busiest men in town.

At this stage, we had a serious discussion on how to coauthor this book. We decided Sharon would focus on history, and Shelley would handle the haunted stories. We'd combine our finds as we put the book together.

Our next step was to gather stories—which presented a logistical problem, as we both live in Baraboo. We needed to get to know Portage and have the townsfolk get to know us and hear about our project. Cook Street seemed the place to start. We visited stores and introduced ourselves. People seemed interested and pleased that we'd be making Portage the star of our book. However, not many people were willing to share their otherworldly experiences. We had to build trust.

We returned to Portage with copies of Shelley and Gwen's *Haunted Baraboo*. Seeing the book seemed to make our project real, and our credibility grew. Gradually, and sometimes almost by accident, we began to gather stories.

A stop at the Chamber of Commerce brought a wonderful surprise. Brad and Marianne were both delighted to suggest people we should talk to—which, of course, included Judy. Those contacts led to quite a few stories. Because of our schedules and the schedules of the people we wanted to talk to, many of those initial interviews were done by phone. Although people were willing to explain their experiences and have us include what happened to them in the book, most of them preferred to remain anonymous. Those whose names have been changed are marked with an asterisk throughout the book.

Eventually, we heard from Fred Galley at Galley Studio. We were a little stunned when we were given an appointment in late fall. Not having kids in high school, we'd forgotten his calendar would be filled with kids needing school pictures. Finally, the day came when he greeted us at the studio. We were quite pleased to meet him and see the mound of photo albums he set out for us to look through. His running commentary on Portage history provided bits and pieces we might have missed completely, like Agoston Haraszthy, who proved to be one of the more unique side stories in the book.

Who would have guessed that the father of the California wine industry planted roots (of grapevines) in Wisconsin?

During the year that we worked on the book, we took almost weekly trips to Portage. On one visit, we toured the Museum at the Portage and marveled at the beauty of Zona Gale's final home. The exhibits helped us understand the complexity of Portage's history. As we continued our research, the museum's *Tales of Old Portage*, which is a compilation of the newspaper articles written by Dorothy McCarthy for the *Portage Daily Register*, and *Portage, A Sesquicentennial History* by Michael J. Goc became important sources of information. We also spent hours at the Portage library going through their history files. The staff there welcomed us and were wonderfully supportive.

We were well aware that other people had written books about hauntings and included Portage in their reports. Those books became another valuable source of information. However, many of the stories we found couldn't be verified. We felt they should still be included, which is why the book has a section called "Murder, Myths and Lore."

As we pulled the book together, we were amazed to find that although the center of Portage contains a large percentage of historic buildings, we gathered very few ghost stories there. The countryside farmhouses provided the majority of the stories for the book. Perhaps the buildings downtown had so many residents that most of them moved on, or maybe those who linger are quieter than those outside of town. We did find a great many cemeteries that are hotbeds of activity. Every book has surprises; even we were surprised. We hope our readers will be surprised by some of the stories, comforted by others, perplexed by some and maybe get an involuntary shiver as they discover what we uncovered.

If you are reading this and have stories of hauntings and unseen visitors in Portage, we would love to hear from you. You never know, there could be a second book. You can email them to barabootours@yahoo.com. Until we meet or speak again, happy hauntings!

PART I
EARLY DAYS AT THE PORTAGE

THE LAND BETWEEN THE RIVERS

Before recorded time, Wisconsin was covered with thick forests and vast grassy prairies. Rivers were thoroughfares taking people and their belongings from place to place as they moved across the landscape. Native Americans used these fluid roads to travel from Lake Michigan to the Gulf of Mexico. A small area of marshy ground made traveling those enormous distances possible.

Wisconsin's two major rivers, the Wisconsin River and the Fox River, almost meet at what is now the city of Portage. The Fox River connected the area to Green Bay and all that is north and east. The Wisconsin River took travelers to the Mississippi and its tributaries.

The land between the Fox and Wisconsin Rivers was uneven, and rattlesnakes lived there. This unique strip was described as low and marshy with clumps of trees toward the middle where the ground was higher. Native Americans carried their canoes and belongings across it. Using this passageway allowed them to move north, south, east and west as they traveled and traded.

In 1634, the French explorer Jean Nicolet crossed Lake Michigan and landed on the shore of Green Bay. His explorations of the area led him to the passage between the Fox and Wisconsin Rivers. He used the French word *portage* to describe the process of carrying boats and supplies from one

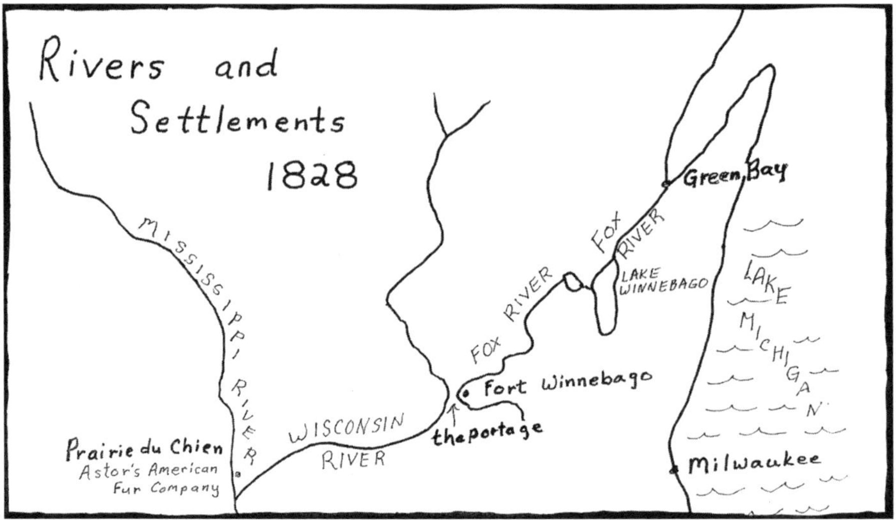

When rivers were roads, the strip of land between the Fox and Wisconsin Rivers allowed travelers to reach Lake Michigan or the Mississippi River. *Sketch by Sharon Hart Addy.*

river to the other. In June 1673, Pierre Marquette and Louis Joliet recorded doing a portage at this site. By the 1780s, it had become a rendezvous spot to trade furs and supplies.

Native Americans called the area Wau-wau-o-nah, meaning the place where a traveler carries his canoe on his back. The Native American name lives on as "Wauona Trail" on the south side of Portage. The street runs east and west, connecting Highway 51 and Highway 33, following the route of the Native American passageway.

THE HOUSE ON WAUONA TRAIL

Habitat for Humanity has been in the Portage area since 2016. The organization began in Americus, Georgia, in 1976. Millard and Linda Fuller developed the concept of "partnership housing" and, with the help of the community, built the first house for Beau and Emma. When former President Jimmy Carter and his wife, Rosalynn, stepped in to support this project, it took off. Habitat for Humanity is now located in all fifty states.

A house on Wauona Trail was a Habitat for Humanity project. Two condemned houses were brought to Portage and combined to create one house. The family who moved in was happy to live there, but soon after settling in, they noticed their home had extra residents.

One night, the family decided to watch a movie. They were all sitting in the living room when they heard footsteps upstairs in their son's room. Someone was walking back and forth. When the dad went up to investigate, he found nothing and came downstairs. The family started to watch their movie again, only to hear the footsteps a few minutes later.

A few weeks later, the son was in his room playing video games. He heard a noise and looked up to see the empty snack bowl on his dresser spinning as if an unseen hand was turning the bowl.

The family sensed the presence of three spirits. One is a spirit they refer to as "Little Grandma." She's warm and loving. She seems to be connected to the family. The other two entities are not known. The family feels that one is residual energy. According to the Travel Channel's paranormal glossary, residual energy is "paranormal activity resulting from the energy imprint of a person or event in time. This could be a place memory or a residual loop of smells, sounds and noise. Residual energy is emotional energy that can be imprinted by a living or crossed over person. It can attach to clothes, furniture, objects and places. These strong emotions stay with the item or site and sometimes reappear as residual loops." The family suspects the pacer in their house is residual energy. The spirit, which they feel is male, tends to pace in the same spot at about the same time. The remaining spirit is an intelligent being. It seems to interact with the family and is playful. Keys go missing, only to end up in a totally different spot. The family has lived in this house for years and intends to continue living there. A few extra inhabitants haven't bothered them yet.

Settlement, Murder and Surrender

French voyageurs made use of "Le Portage" as they traded knives, blankets, cloth, combs, mirrors, guns and whiskey for furs trapped by Native Americans. Unloading the canoes and carrying them and their cargo across the two-mile portage took a full day, according to research contained in the book *A Man Called Baraboo: The Life and Travels of an 18th Century Voyageur* by M. Richard Tully. The canoe used by Baraboo, whose name was originally spelled Barbeau, was about twenty feet long and three or four feet wide. It was made of thick birchbark on a frame of cedarwood. The bark was sewn together with fir tree roots, and all the seams were gummed. Each time Barbeau and his crew of six went ashore, they had to secure the canoe far enough away from land so it wouldn't be damaged by shoreline rocks or other hazards, and then they had to unload it. The fragile craft couldn't hold the weight of the cargo without the support of the water under it.

Pierre Pauquette, an early resident of the Portage area, ran a trading post and acted as an interpreter during government transactions with Native Americans. *Fred Galley Collection.*

In the early 1790s, a French voyageur named Laurent Barth recognized a business opportunity. The boats used by traders had become too large to be carried easily from one river to the other. Barth built a cabin for his family and thereby became the first European resident of Portage. He made a good living hauling boats between the rivers on long wagons pulled by horses. Other entrepreneurs followed his example, but not all of them were honest. John Jacob Astor, whose American Fur Trading Company was headquartered in Prairie du Chien on the Mississippi River, sent Pierre Pauquette to establish a trading post at the portage to handle the company's shipments across the swampy divide.

Pauquette, described as a tall, strong, vigorous man with Ho Chunk features, was one of the most well-respected people during the early days of Portage. He was born near St. Louis in 1795. His father was French and his mother Winnebago, which is what the Ho Chunk were called at the time. Along with his trapping and trading skills, Pauquette was known for his honesty and integrity. Although he never learned to read or write, he was trusted to keep accounts in his head for many of the men he worked with. Pauquette, who spoke French, Ho Chunk and English, negotiated with local Native Americans and other settlers involved in transporting beaver, fox and other furs across the portage between the Wisconsin and Fox Rivers. In addition to running Astor's fur trading post on the Fox River, Pauquette also formed his own business, ferrying people and goods across the Wisconsin River. He was a well-respected interpreter for the Ho Chunk in their dealings with the government.

Disputes between Native Americans and European settlers increased as lead miners from the East moved into Ho Chunk land in the southwest corner of Wisconsin. Anger and revenge, fed by misunderstandings and

An artist's rendering of Native American dwellings and canoes along the river. *Fred Galley Collection.*

rumors, flared on both sides. The clash led to the murder of a settler's family near Fort Crawford on the Mississippi. The U.S. Army's reaction was swift. The Ho Chunk band, including Red Bird, who was a war chief, and We Kaw, who had participated in the raid near Fort Crawford, fled east toward the portage. Militia under the command of Major William Whistler moved south from Green Bay and set up camp at what would become the site of Fort Winnebago. Their orders were to hold the crucial portage between the Fox and Wisconsin.

The American troops had only been in their temporary quarters for about a day when a delegation of Ho Chunk including Chief Naw Kaw approached the army encampment. Through an interpreter, who might have been Pauquette, the Ho Chunk stated that Red Bird and We Kaw would surrender the next day if the army would not attack the Ho Chunk who were gathered nearby. Whistler and his advisors agreed.

True to their word, the next day, September 3, 1827, Red Bird, Chief Naw Kaw and their followers approached the soldiers' camp on foot and horseback. When they were near the river, they broke into a death dirge. The

Chief Red Bird surrendered with great dignity. *Fred Galley Collection.*

military, hearing the mournful song, thought it was a war chant and readied their guns. The Ho Chunk stopped on a ridge over the river, and Chief Naw Kaw moved forward. He spoke to the government's Indian agents, asking that Red Bird and We Kaw be treated with dignity, like braves surrendering willingly, and not be put in irons. The agents conferred with Commander Whistler, who accepted the terms.

When Whistler moved forward to greet Red Bird, he was flanked by two companies of regular infantry men standing at arms, a military band and those Native Americans who were allied with the U.S. government. Red Bird and We Kaw stepped from the gathering of Ho Chunk. Red Bird was dressed in white elk skin leather with a square of red cloth on his chest. In his left hand he held an ornamental pipe; in his right hand he held a white flag. He moved forward with great dignity, knowing his surrender would prevent a massacre of his people but that he would lose his liberty and his life.

After Red Bird surrendered, the government, fearing other uprisings, felt it necessary to strengthen the military presence in the eastern side of what is now Wisconsin. In 1828, soldiers were dispatched to build Fort Winnebago at the portage.

A hill rising on the eastern side of the Fox River became the site of temporary barracks for the troops. Wood was the common building material of the day. The marshes near present-day Portage provided an abundance of tamarack, and it was used for these first buildings. Tamarack is rot resistant, which makes it an excellent material for posts, poles, mine timbers, railroad ties and pulp for paper.

Fort Winnebago on the eastern shore of the Fox River was built to protect the portage. *Fred Galley Collection.*

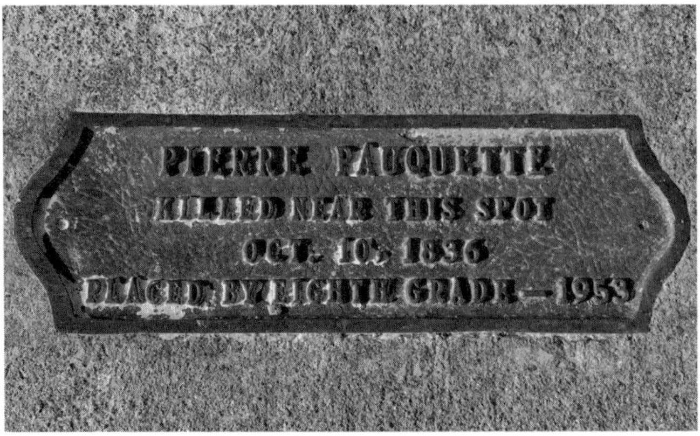

A brass plaque marks the spot where Pierre Pauquette was murdered by a disgruntled tribesman. *Photo by Shelley Mordini.*

By the fall of 1828, two quickly constructed barracks of tamarack logs had been erected at the fort's site. During that first winter, a delegation of soldiers was sent fifty miles north to the Yellow River to cut pine trees. When spring came, these military lumberjacks floated the logs down the Wisconsin River to a landing spot near the portage and then hauled them to the site of the fort. There they cut and planed the logs, shaping and smoothing them into the lumber needed to create the fort's buildings.

Pierre Pauquette continued as a friend and interpreter for the Ho Chunk. On October 10, 1836, he was on his way home after several days of negotiations between the Ho Chunk and government representatives about the acquisition of Ho Chunk land. As he and friends approached his boat landing on the Wisconsin River, he was confronted by a disgruntled tribesman and shot. A plaque marking the spot where he died is embedded in the sidewalk near the flagpole at the corner of West Cook and MacFarlane Road. Pauquette Park is named in his honor.

FORT WINNEBAGO AND THE SURGEON'S QUARTERS

The site for Fort Winnebago was selected carefully. The land chosen was bordered on three sides by the Fox River and across from the eastern end of the portage. The four thousand acres chosen for the fort encompassed Frances Le Roy's house, which the government purchased.

Le Roy's French-style house is U-shaped. It looks like two buildings joined by a recessed passageway. The exterior consists of hand-hewn square pine logs, dovetailed at the corners. Inside, tamarack culled from nearby swamps

The Fort Winnebago Surgeon's Quarters, built in about 1820, was restored and is maintained as a museum by the Daughters of the American Revolution. *Photo by Sharon Hart Addy.*

makes up the timbers supporting the floors and ceilings of the four large rooms on the first floor. In 1834, the walls were lathed and plastered and the floorboards probably replaced. Today, we know the building as the Fort Winnebago Surgeon's Quarters.

The Fort Winnebago Surgeon's Quarters was built about 1820 by the Le Roy family on high ground overlooking the portage trail. The Le Roys ran a successful business moving canoes and cargo from the Fox to the Wisconsin River. In 1817, they charged ten dollars to carry a canoe that normally held five men. For each one hundred pounds of cargo, they charged fifty cents.

After the Le Roys sold the house to the U.S. Army, it was assigned to a sutler, a civilian who sells provisions. An enterprising teenager named Satterlee Clark was appointed as the sutler. Because of his young age, Clark had to hire an older man to work with him so he could run the store. Clark was in charge of the store for several years before the fort commander closed it. The building was needed for another use.

The fort's original hospital had become too small. A larger one was built close to the Le Roy house, and the house was assigned as living quarters for the hospital's surgeon. The building became known as the Surgeon's Quarters.

The September 20, 2022 Ghost Tour

In September 2022, Baraboo Tours and Shelley Mordini were asked by the Daughters of the American Revolution, the group that manages the Fort Winnebago Surgeon's Quarters, to conduct a ghost tour. The staff of Baraboo Tours brought dowsing rods, an ovilus (a machine that produces words using white noise), ghost meter pros and flashlights. Twenty people signed up to participate in this ghost tour.

The building is not wired for electricity, and no candles or lanterns were lit to provide light. In a semi-dark room in the Surgeon's Quarters, the activity began when the ovilus spit out the word *whiskey*. The team hadn't brought whiskey with them. They texted a friend, who brought them a small bottle of brandy. The spirits seemed appeased by the alcohol and produced more words: *surgeon*, *arm* and *major*. Small sounds were heard in the Surgeon's Quarters but nothing identifiable. The group left the Surgeon's Quarters and walked to the old schoolhouse, which had been moved to the grounds near the Surgeon's Quarters. In the schoolhouse, they heard several small noises. The most notable sound was the door of the potbelly stove being swung closed with loud clang. The noise startled many people in the group.

The July 2023 Visit

Shelley and the Baraboo Haunted Tours staff were invited to return to the Surgeon's Quarters and conduct a haunted tour in July 2023. The staff was better prepared this time, bringing dowsing rods, an ovilus, ghost meter pros, flashlights, whiskey and a small glass. Forty people attended the session.

The entrance to the Surgeon's Quarters is in the middle of the hallway that connects the two parts of the building. The section to the left includes the surgeon's operating room with a fireplace against the interior wall. The original operating table is near a window in this room. Near the table, the floor has a depression in the shape of a man's right footprint. The reason it was formed is unknown. The small room next to the operating room is furnished with a bed and chest that are original artifacts. This room does not connect with the entryway.

To the right of the entrance hall, there are two more rooms. One is a large gathering area, similar to today's living room, with a big fireplace and many wooden chairs. The room at the front of this side of the building is the original kitchen with a large hearth. A small door next to the fireplace opens to a narrow set of steep stairs that twist to go behind the fireplace and end in the attic. The stairs are no longer stable, so the attic is inaccessible to the public. Here's what happened the evening Shelley and her team visited:

> *The group gathered that warm, dark evening in the operating room. The building has no air conditioning or electricity. Flashlights were the only illumination. Although the night started out without a lot of evidence of paranormal activity, some words came through.*
>
> *While in the Surgeon's Quarters' kitchen, the team brought out their supply of bourbon and poured a small amount into a hand-blown glass. The ovilus picked up many words, but no one noticed any movement. Not wanting to carry the bottle and partly filled glass, Shelley asked for a volunteer to drink the bourbon. The volunteer drank the whiskey, and Shelley placed the bottle and empty glass on a table in the hallway near the building's front door. Then she led the group to the schoolhouse, a short walk away from the Surgeon's Quarters.*
>
> *After a few minutes in the schoolhouse, Shelley asked her assistant to go back to the Surgeon's Quarters and set the whiskey bottle and glass on the surgeon's table. She planned to take the group there again after a few minutes in the school. The assistant went off to move the bottle and glass. A few minutes later, she came back to ask Shelley where she left the glass and bourbon bottle. The guest who drank the bourbon and watched Shelley put the bottle and glass near the doorway volunteered to go over to the Surgeon's Quarters with the assistant and help her locate them. After a few minutes, they both came running back to the school and called Shelley outside. They asked her exactly where she'd left the bottle and glass. Shelley said they were on the small table by the front door. The two turned, stared at each other and said, "That's not where it is."*
>
> *Shelley gathered the group and led them back to the Surgeon's Quarters. Inside the front door, she looked at the empty spot where she'd left the bourbon and glass. The assistant and the volunteer pointed shaky fingers into the surgeon's operating room. The bourbon bottle and glass were sitting on the surgeon's table, positioned as if the surgeon intended to use them for his next patient.*

Whiskey was a popular way of numbing patients before surgery. In the late 1800s, anesthesia as we know it today hadn't been invented. Alcohol was used to help deaden pain and numb the patient for surgery. The need

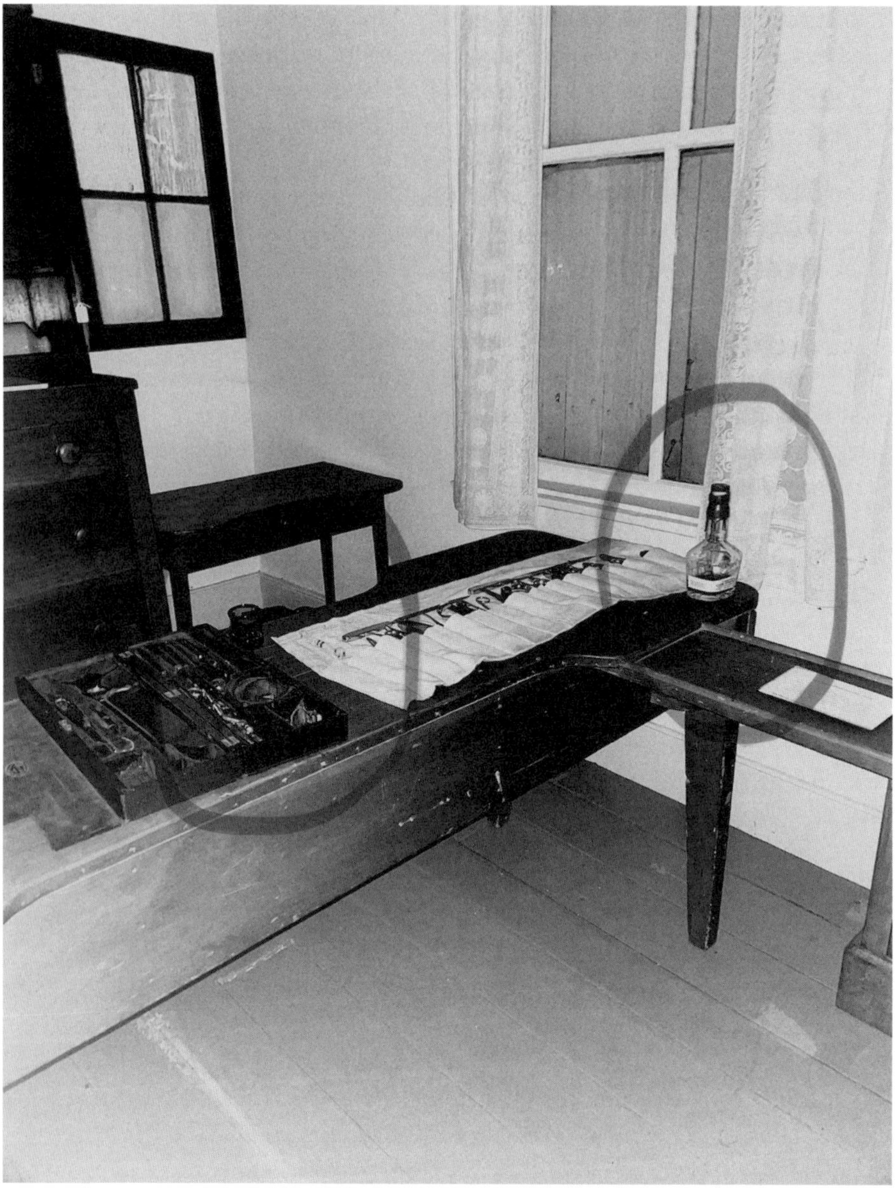

Above: The bottle of whiskey and glass were moved to where the surgeon would have put them before an operation. *Photo by Shelley Mordini.*

Opposite: Veterans of eight wars are buried in Fort Winnebago's Cemetery. Cooper Pixley's headstone survived fires that burned wooden markers. *Photo by Shelley Mordini.*

for sterile conditions was also unknown at the time. The fact that germs and viruses cause infections and illness hadn't been definitively established, so not all medical professionals thought they needed to wash their hands or instruments before operating. Infections caused by nonsterile conditions sometimes led to death.

Most of the medical needs the fort's surgeon attended to were related to normal illnesses and diseases, not battle wounds. There were no major battles around the fort, although soldiers from the fort were sent to areas of conflict.

Those who died were buried in the Fort Winnebago Cemetery. The "Burial Ground," as it was called at the time it was established, is one of the oldest cemeteries in the state. It became the resting place for fort personnel, their families and settlers who lived in the area. Some Native Americans were also buried there.

Seventy-five graves dot the Fort Winnebago Cemetery. It was established in 1828, and interments began in 1835. A granite boulder on the grounds is a monument to the unknown dead. A separate monument marks the site where Chief Red Wing surrendered in 1827.

Today, the cemetery's fence encloses about two acres. Once, the cemetery was much larger. When the first burials took place in the 1830s, wooden headboards marked the graves. The top of the headboard was painted black to indicate the deceased had been a member of the military. A few graves had stone markers. When a fire swept through the cemetery, all the wooden headboards burned, leaving only the stone markers. A wooden fence was built around those headstones. When the fence burned in another fire, an iron fence was erected around the remaining graves. For years farmers tilling fields near the cemetery turned up wooden caskets spilling skeletons.

Today's visitors to the fort cemetery will find veterans of eight wars buried there: the Revolutionary War, the War of 1812, the Blackhawk War, the Seminole War, the War Between the States, the Mexican War, the Spanish-American War and World War I.

Two graves honor the remains of veterans who served during the Revolutionary War (1775–83). The body of Alexander Porter was moved from his first burial site in Freedom, New York, when that cemetery was abandoned. His great-grandson, whose family settled in the Portage area, arranged the transfer to the fort's cemetery. The other veteran, Cooper Pixley, was a Portage resident. He died in 1855 when he was eighty-six. He was born in 1769, just six years before the start of the Revolutionary War. Although he was only fourteen when it ended, he served during the war. He may have been part of a fife and drum unit that set the pace during marches or was a camp helper. Perhaps he did both. He may even have carried a rifle.

Today, only the cemetery and the Surgeon's Quarters are left of what was once the four-thousand-acre government claim. The original plan included space for vegetable gardens, cattle grounds, barns and workshops of various kinds as well as barracks, the guard house, a hospital, washhouses, a magazine where munitions were stored, an ordnance store containing military supplies, a subsistence store, the sutter's store (a sutter was a civilian allowed to run a store on or near an army post), the officers' quarters and the fort's offices.

By a strange twist of fate, one of the officers who helped establish and build Fort Winnebago was also instrumental in decommissioning it. A recent graduate of West Point, Jefferson Davis was a second lieutenant when he was sent to the wilderness that became Wisconsin. He arrived on the shore of the Fox River with the plans for Fort Winnebago. During the two years Davis was attached to the fort, he was in charge of construction and carpentry. In 1831, he was transferred to Fort Crawford and served during the Blackhawk War. As peace settled across the area, Fort Winnebago became unnecessary. After having soldiers garrisoned there for seventeen years, the fort was evacuated in 1845. A disastrous fire in March 1856 destroyed most of the buildings. Jefferson Davis, as U.S. secretary of war, signed the order to sell whatever was left of the fort he helped to build. In yet another twist in his career, Davis resigned as a state senator from Mississippi to become president of the Confederacy.

Although the fire destroyed most of the fort's buildings, folks living nearby salvaged usable materials. Lumber and brick scattered across the area and were incorporated into buildings and farms. The Surgeon's Quarters survived the fire and continued to provide housing at times to farmers, newcomers or laborers. Eventually, it was empty and in disrepair. During the Great Depression of the 1930s, squatters used some of the building's materials as firewood. At that point, the Wau Bun Chapter of the Daughters

FORT WINNEBAGO IN 1830

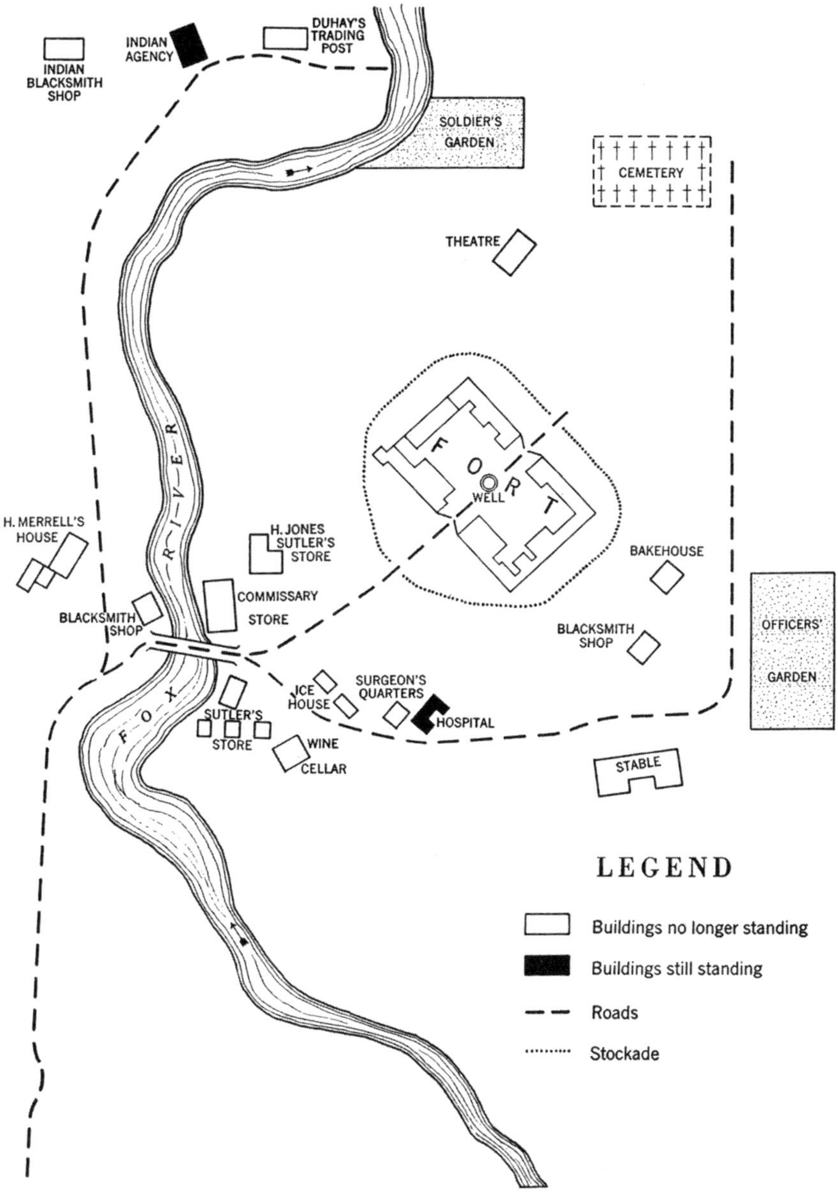

Fort Winnebago encompassed four thousand acres on the Fox River. An outpost of civilization, it provided everything needed to sustain the military. *Fred Galley Collection.*

of the American Revolution, aware of the building's historical significance, purchased the building. Under their care, the Surgeon's Quarters was restored. It opened to the public in 1954.

THE SOLDIER IN BLUE

A property as old and extensive as the Surgeon's Quarters requires a lot of maintenance. The assistance of volunteers is welcome. Steven* and his wife, Maria*, believed in giving back to the community. Steven enjoyed working outdoors, so he offered to help with the landscaping at Fort Winnebago Surgeon's Quarters.

He'd been cutting the grass for several months and had a routine worked out. Because the lawn in front of the buildings slopes down to a little rise near the river, he walked across the hill, parallel to the buildings, as he cut the grass.

One lovely evening in mid-July, he'd cut about half the lawn when he heard a loud bang, like a door slamming. Startled, he looked around. As far as he knew, he was the only one on the property. In the graying light of dusk, he didn't see anyone, and the buildings looked the way they always did. He assumed the bang he heard was a noise from nearby and went back to work. He finished cutting to the edge of the property and turned to cut across the lawn again.

He was near the front of the Surgeon's Quarters when he saw a soldier in a blue uniform jacket, wearing a flat uniform cap and carrying a rifle with a bayonet. The young man started down the sloping lawn as if he'd just left the building. He was tall with dark hair, and he looked about twenty years old. He walked in a straight line and was about to cross the path of the mower.

Stunned, Steven stopped and watched as the soldier walked within a foot or so of the front of the mower. The young man didn't look left or right. He seemed completely unaware that Steven and the lawnmower were there. He continued down the lawn to the rise along the riverbank, went up that small hill and disappeared. Steven left his mower and ran to see where the soldier had gone. He wasn't anywhere.

The experience was too much to believe. Steven thought he was going crazy. He was so shaken up that for three days, he kept what he saw to himself. Then, finally, he told Maria, who was just as astounded and amazed as he was.

The Indian Agency House

The Indian Agency House, built in 1832, was the home of the United States government's Indian Agent John Harris Kinzie and his wife, Juliette. He was sent to handle the relationships between the Native Americans and the government. He also distributed the annual payments made to Native Americans for the sale of their land. In addition, he was the fort's postmaster.

The Indian Agency House quickly became a social center for the fort. The Kinzies' visitors included officers, travelers passing through the area and Native Americans who came to the Kinzies when they needed advice or were in trouble. In her book *Wau-Bun*, Juliette M. Kinzie describes life on the frontier and the people she and her husband met during the eight months they lived in the house.

In 1833, John Kinzie left the service and moved to the Chicago area. The commander of the fort took over Kinzie's duties as Indian agent and postmaster. Because the commander didn't need housing, the house was rented. James Ubaldine and his wife turned it into a tavern. The fort's soldiers were among their best customers, but the whiskey they drank led to unruly

The Indian Agency House, rescued and maintained by the Colonial Dames of America, was built in 1832. *Fred Galley Collection.*

behavior, which created discipline problems at the fort. The tavern didn't last long. The next resident, Satterlee Clark, made the house a trading post. The trading post closed in 1840 when the Native Americans were sent from the area. Then the house became the home of Captain Gideon Low and his wife. After Captain Low died, his wife needed a way to support herself. For income, she rented her extra bedrooms. She ran the boardinghouse with the help of two Black servants, James and Eliza Low, who apparently adopted the family name. After her death, the property was used as a farm. For long stretches of time, the house sat empty. The Colonial Dames of America in the State of Wisconsin purchased the rundown property and restored it. In 1933, 101 years after it was built, the Kinzie house was opened to the public.

There are very few stories of people encountering visitors from the past in the house or on the grounds. Perhaps this is because those who lived there moved on; perhaps it's because telling tales of unusual events in the house or on the property is discouraged. However, some tales have been told.

ASHY FOOTPRINTS

The two-story house has an entryway with stairs going up to the second-floor bedrooms. A hallway next to the steps leads to a small room behind the stairs that might have been an office. What we would call the living room or parlor is at the front of the house to the right of the stairs and the hallway. The dining room and then the kitchen are behind the living room. In the kitchen, a large fireplace dominates the exterior wall. The fireplace is fitted with a spit and the cast-iron cooking pots used in the 1800s. Docents welcome visitors, show them through the house and talk about the furnishings.

Jane* was one of those docents. She enjoyed working in the house but was puzzled by what she'd find when she unlocked the house in the morning: ashy footprints leading away from the fireplace. She'd sweep them up before she left the kitchen to check the other rooms.

When she returned to the kitchen, the footprints would be there again. She knew she'd swept them up, and she knew she didn't make them. Whose could they be? They could belong to someone from the Kinzies' time in the house or from any of the other people who lived in it during its history. There's no way to connect them with a period.

In the morning, the docent found ashy footprints leading away from the fireplace. *Illustration by Brett Kawitter.*

HOT SPOTS

Chris Okan of Spirit Investigating Ghost Hunting Twins, who researched hauntings in the area, was invited to conduct an investigation at the Indian Agency House. A group of community members attended. Although Okan didn't record any incidents or connections in the house, his K-2 meter, which measures electrical output, found two hot spots while he walked the grounds. He speculated that these hot spots indicate graves, but there are

Juliette Kinzie wrote about her experiences on the frontier and life at the Indian Agency House in her book *Wau-Bun*. *Fred Galley Collection.*

no markers identifying burials; however, the hot spots show that spirits are still in the area.

The Indian Agency House continues to be administered and cared for by the National Society of the Colonial Dames of America in the State of Wisconsin. It's open for visitors during the summer. Juliette Kinzie's book *Wau-Bun*, which details her travels and experiences in the territorial days, is available there.

EVEN BEFORE THE KINZIES moved away, there were discussions about replacing the portage with a canal. The idea generated a lot of interest. An attempt to dig the canal by hand in 1835 failed. Travelers, voyagers and traders continued to portage their canoes between the Fox and Wisconsin Rivers.

A warehouse stood at the Fox River end of the portage, with the sutter's store and a tavern nearby. The word "tavern" had a different meaning in the 1800s. Taverns were boardinghouses offering food and lodging. The fort's village included a post office, grocery store, blacksmith, gristmill and homes. The community around the fort reached north to include the Indian Agency House and the American Fur Company Post.

Part II
Hauntings from the Stagecoach Era

Fort Winnebago and the Indian Agency House drew people to the growing settlement around the fort. Clusters of buildings offering shelter, food and necessities developed near the fort and along the river. Soldiers, supply wagons, fur traders and visitors arrived at the fort and sometimes stayed. Native Americans gathered to conduct business with the U.S. government. However, getting to the fort wasn't easy. Traveling on rivers or trails through the forests and prairies was difficult and, at times, impossible. The trails were often hard to follow, and they didn't accommodate wheeled vehicles. Solid roads wide enough for wagons were needed. As the government struggled for greater control of the Territory of Wisconsin, the ability to move troops and supplies quickly became more important.

The army put soldiers to work creating a Military Road to connect the territory's major forts, Fort Howard and Fort Crawford. Fort Howard sat near the place where the Fox River and Lake Michigan's Green Bay meet. Fort Crawford was close to Prairie du Chien, where the Wisconsin River empties into the Mississippi River. Fort Winnebago and the important strip of land linking the Fox and Wisconsin Rivers sat in the middle.

Many sections of the roads built during this period followed Native American trails. In the forest, trails were marked by cutting a hand-sized piece of bark off trees along the way. This was called "blazing." In prairies, mounds of earth or piles of stones marked the way. Creating thoroughfares through marshes and lowlands necessitated building a base for vehicles to travel on. Corduroy and plank roads were built. To create a corduroy road, logs were laid crosswise, creating a rough but stable roadway. They were

In the mid-1800s, Cook Street became the business center for Portage. *Fred Galley Collection.*

called corduroy roads because of the resemblance to the ridges of corduroy cloth. To smooth the ride, sand or dirt was used to fill the spaces between the logs. Plank roads produced a smoother ride and resembled boardwalks. Small logs were laid lengthwise like railroad tracks and were topped with planks going across the width.

Although roads helped, weather added to the challenge of traveling. Spring thaws and autumn rains reduced dirt roads to muddy treks. In winter, snowstorms and snowdrifts became obstacles. There were no shelters, no stores, no place and no one to turn to for help, and there was always a chance of encountering wild animals.

The inconvenience of carrying canoes and cargo across the Wauona Trail between the Fox and Wisconsin Rivers led to reoccurring conversations about building a canal to replace the trail. The advantages included being able to use the waterway all year and having enough depth and width to allow steamboats and other watercraft to move easily. Digging the canal began, by hand, in 1835. The initial attempt failed, but the idea was never completely abandoned.

When Wisconsin became a territory in 1836, Portage became a boomtown. Visitors and settlers came over land and by river. During these early years of settlement, the fort and those living near it relied on local craftsmen: the blacksmith, cooper, gunsmith, cabinetmaker, cobbler, wagonmaker, baker and other specialists. Road improvements led to stagecoach travel.

Stagecoach routes radiating from Chicago spread throughout the Midwest. The coaches carried goods and passengers, but their most lucrative and

Wells Fargo's Concord coaches were the top of the line in comfort. Passengers swayed gently as they rode. *Courtesy of Wells Fargo.*

important cargo was the U.S. mail. Mail pouches were stacked in the boot, the leather-covered storage area at the back of the coach. If there was room, passengers' luggage was stowed there too. When the boot was full, luggage went on top of the coach or was put inside, where it sat on the coach floor under the passengers' feet. If there was no room on the floor, passengers held their bags on their laps.

Stagecoach travel was not for the faint-hearted. The bright red Concord coaches that became the symbol of Wells Fargo were the top of the line in comfort. The coach's passenger compartment was attached to the undercarriage by belts made of bull hide. As horses, running all out, pulled the coach along the dirt roads, passengers experienced a rocking motion. However, not all stage lines used the expensive Concord coaches.

In other coaches, the body rested on steel springs, and passengers felt every rut and stone the vehicle encountered. Dust was another problem. Windows were simply openings. Pulling down the windows' shades didn't stop the dust flying from the churning wheels. It billowed into the coach, causing some passengers to hold scarfs or handkerchiefs over their mouths and noses. Some coaches had three rows of seats. Two rows faced each other, forcing three people to ride backward. The third seat was a backless bench between the two rows. The best seats were on the top, away from road dust and the proximity of other—perhaps unsavory or unwashed—passengers. Stagecoach lines enforced rules that included not talking about highwaymen or robberies (so women and children wouldn't be frightened) and not leaning on fellow passengers while you were sleeping. Every ten or twelve miles, stages stopped to change the horses, which ran the entire distance. Inns at stagecoach stops offered quick food. However, if you weren't on the coach when the fresh horses were ready to go, you missed your ride and might have to wait a day to catch another coach.

The Old Stagecoach Stop

One of the oldest houses on Franklin Street was a stagecoach stop. Now it's an apartment building. Elise* lives in one of the apartments. She's aware of a little girl with dark hair who wears a white frilly dress. Elise has also seen an older man, and she senses two other spirits in the building. But she more than senses them; they're an active presence. During the winter, she turns the heat down to sixty-eight degrees before she goes to bed. In the morning, she finds the temperature is set at seventy-four. The temperature never stays lower than seventy-four very long, and it never goes higher than seventy-four. Not even on hot summer days.

Elise enjoys computer games. She plays them with a screen and projector. At night, she turns them off. Several times a week, she finds the projector is on when she gets up in the morning. Her unseen roommates seem to have their preferences.

The Helpful Maid

In one of the older homes in town, which might have been an inn or a boardinghouse in the early days of Portage, a young woman was hired to do light housekeeping. She was preparing to dust by moving everything off the top of a dresser to a small bedside table. When she heard her cellphone ringing in another room, she left everything on the table and exited the room to answer her phone. When she got back to the bedroom, everything she'd moved was back on the top of the dresser, exactly where it had been before she moved it, and the room smelled of roses.

Being a polite and appreciative young woman, she thanked her unseen helper. Whoever it was didn't limit her visits to the bedroom. Sometimes the young woman caught the scent in other parts of the house. She came to think of the spirit as Rose and guessed she'd been a maid in another, earlier, time.

The Traveler in the Top Hat

Lori* and her family moved to Portage in 1932. Lori's father managed a store in Chicago and was offered the job of managing a new store in Portage. He considered it a great opportunity, so he loaded up his family of seven and headed north.

When the family arrived in Portage, they needed a place to live. They hoped to buy a larger house than the one they had in Chicago. They found a former stagecoach stop available for purchase. The house was much grander than the family needed, but the extra space was welcomed for the five children. Lori was the youngest of the children and was probably the most excited about not having to share a room. The new home and city brought much joy to the family. They loved living and working in Portage, especially being close to downtown and their father's workplace. Lori had many fond memories walking down Cook Street as a child.

As the years passed, Lori's brother and sisters moved out of the house to start their lives as adults. Lori stayed with her parents until they died. She inherited the house by default; none of her siblings was interested in owning such a large home. She married a wonderful man from Portage, and they had two beautiful daughters. After the girls grew up, Lori and her husband continued to live in the former stagecoach stop, fixing it up and maintaining it as a beautiful home. In 2010, Lori's husband passed away, leaving Lori by herself in the house.

One night in November of the year her husband died, Lori was sitting in her living room knitting and watching TV. She heard a noise in the front entryway and saw a man about six feet tall walking *through* the front door. He didn't open the door; he just walked through it. He wore a stovepipe hat and a long black overcoat. He had a dark beard and was carrying a

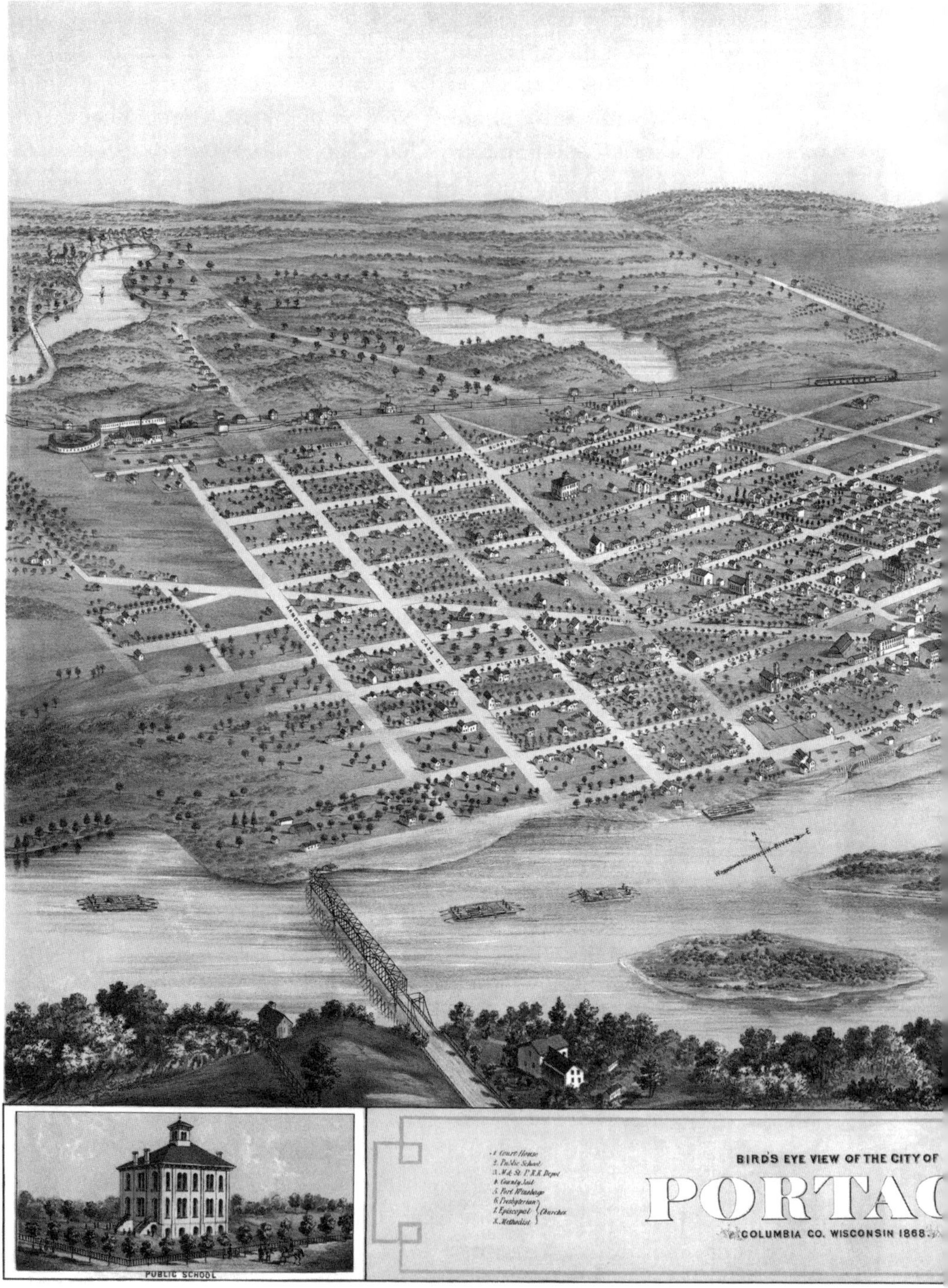
Armstrong St.
Cass St.
Dunn St.
Wisconsin St.
Pleasant St.
Conant St.
Cook St.
Canal St.
PUBLIC SCHOOL
1. Court House
2. Public School
3. M.& St. P. R.R. Depot
4. County Jail
5. Fort Winnebago
6. Presbyterian
7. Episcopal
8. Methodist
Churches
BIRD'S EYE VIEW OF THE CITY OF
PORTAG
COLUMBIA CO. WISCONSIN 1868.

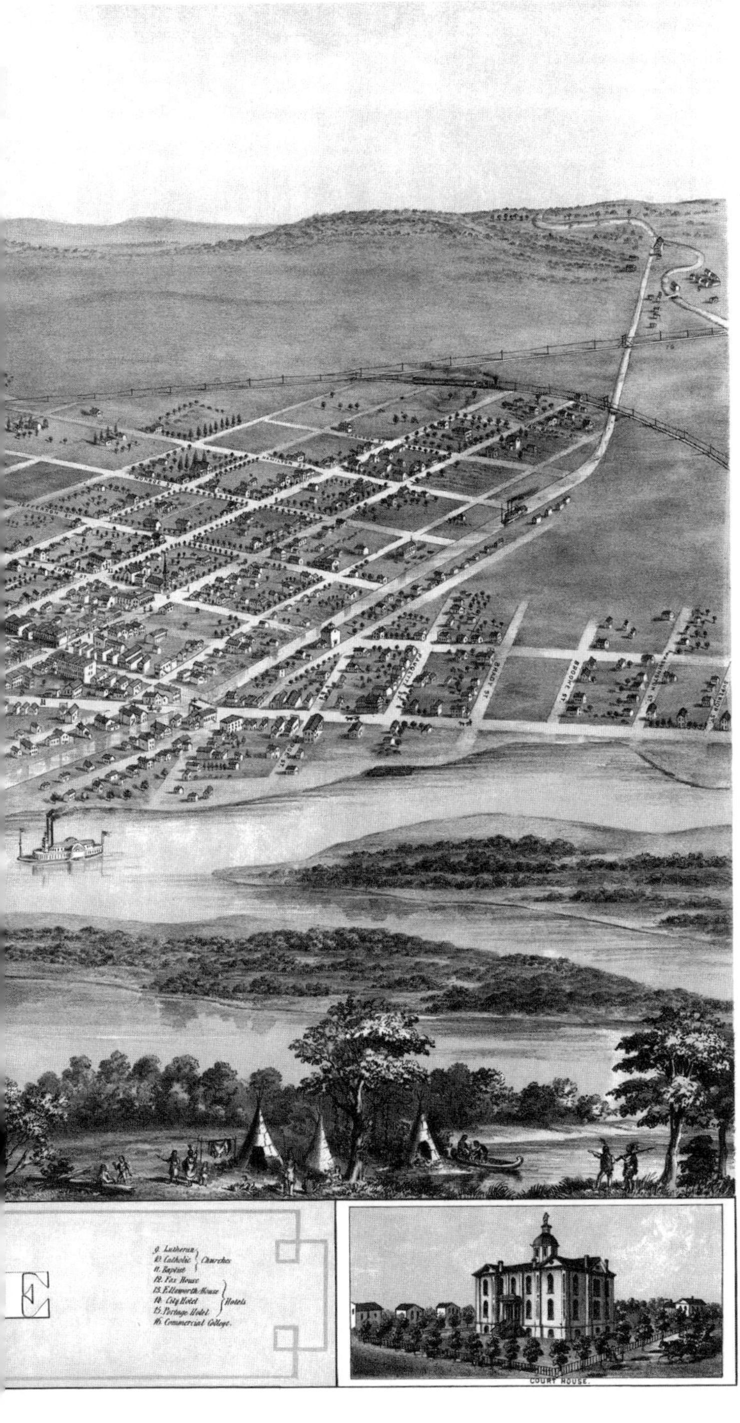

The growing town of Portage stretched between the Wisconsin and Fox Rivers. A canal replaced the pathway between the rivers. *Fred Galley Collection.*

suitcase. He didn't make eye contact with Lori but instead walked through the living room. He disappeared before he entered the kitchen. Startled, Lori simply stared at the spot where he'd vanished. After a few minutes, she told herself she was spending too much time alone and was starting to see things.

The incident upset her so much that the next time she talked to her younger daughter, Cindy*, she mentioned it. The story upset Cindy too, but Cindy was a very practical, down-to-earth gal. She decided to find out what was really going on with her mom. She told her mom she'd come over the next Saturday night and stay with her. Together, they'd see if the gentleman reappeared. Lori liked that idea. She was getting on in age and knew her daughters were discussing putting her into a nursing home. If her mind was starting to go, she knew that's where she'd end up, but if Cindy saw the fellow in the top hat, both Lori and her daughter would know the man wasn't a figment of a failing mind.

Saturday night came. Lori and Cindy were in the living room watching a movie on TV. At 8:15 p.m., they heard a noise at the front door and turned to watch. The man with the stovepipe top hat appeared and stepped through the front door, just as he'd done before. He walked through the living room, passed Lori and Cindy and disappeared before getting to the kitchen.

Lori and Cindy looked at each other. Cindy was astonished. Her eyes were wide open, and her mouth was, too. When she could talk, she said, "Mom, did you see that?" Lori said she did and added that the man did exactly what he had done all the other times she'd seen him. She suggested they finish watching the movie and go to bed. Cindy, stunned, asked her mom, "Go to bed? Are you crazy?" Lori, certain now that she wasn't imagining things, explained, "He never walks through twice."

The next week, Cindy invited a paranormal group to come over to cleanse the house. The traveler wasn't seen after that. Lori passed away in early 2011, roughly a year after her husband died.

From the time Lori's family moved into the house in 1932 until her husband's death in 2010, no one experienced any paranormal activity. Cindy sometimes wonders if the traveler's appearance was a message for her mother, telling her to get her affairs in order because she'd soon be moving to another realm.

FAMOUS TRAVELERS

Count Agoston Haraszthy stayed in Portage as he explored the area. His legacy lives on in Prairie Du Sac. *Fred Galley Collection.*

Stagecoaches brought people from far and wide to Portage. Some settled in and made Portage their home, while others moved on. Hungarian Count Agoston Haraszthy was one of the more unique visitors. He stayed in Portage while he explored the area. After purchasing land along the Wisconsin River, he laid out streets and property plots for Sauk City. In what is now the town of Roxbury, he grew grapes and dug caves into the hillside. Today Wollersheim Winery uses the caves he dug to store their wine. Haraszthy's stay in Wisconsin ended in 1849, when he led a wagon train to California. His interest in grapes and wine led him to establish a vineyard in Sonoma Valley. He's considered by some to be the father of the wine industry in California.

Stagecoaches remained the major mode of travel for nearly a century. The success of the Erie Canal in New York kept the idea of digging a canal between the Fox and Wisconsin Rivers alive. By 1850, the Portage Canal was complete enough to allow some boat traffic. Improvements over the next ten years deepened and widened the waterway so it could accommodate any of the steamboats that used the Fox or Wisconsin Rivers. Unfortunately, steamboats could use the rivers only when the water levels were high. Of course, high water levels after heavy rain or spring flooding created problems, too, as did winter ice.

While engineers worked to improve the canal, railroad companies spread tracks across the countryside. The railroad reached Portage in 1857, bringing more settlers. The city's population grew to 2,879 in 1860. Folks earned a living by working in sawmills, flour mills, hotels and taverns and by shipping goods on flats and barges. Lawyers, doctors, politicians, preachers, newspapermen and other professionals added to the population. Visitors and settlers poured into the city. Business opportunities increased. Two- and

Steam locomotives puffed their way across the country, bringing prosperity in their wake. *Fred Galley Collection.*

three-story buildings were erected along East Cook Street, offering all the necessities of life in a vibrant town.

Portage became such a strategic railroad stop that President Rutherford B. Hayes, his wife and a delegation of forty-six fellow travelers spent a few hours in Portage. They were headed to the East Coast after a tour of the Red River country in North Dakota. At that time, trains didn't include a dining car. Passengers got off, had a meal at the station and then reboarded to continue their trip. President Hayes and his traveling companions ate their breakfast at Portage's Fox House Depot on September 10, 1878. Their special car was attached to the regular 8:00 a.m. train.

Part III
Spirits on Cook Street

As the commercial section of Portage grew, Cook Street became the town's main street. Many of the buildings there were built in the late 1800s and early 1900s and are still in use today. Stores or offices fill the street level. The upper floors are apartments, offices or storage spaces. People from the past linger in some of them.

After-Hours Visitors

In the 100 block of East Cook Street, an artist set up her studio on the second floor of an old building. Her space was near the back steps. While working late one night, she heard footsteps coming up the stairs. She listened, expecting someone to reach her door, but no one arrived. When she looked out, no one was there. But that wasn't the only time she had an unseen caller. The ground-level store has a slightly disguised after-hours doorbell for visitors who stop by when the store is closed. For the convenience of people who have offices or studios on the second floor, the after-hours bell rings upstairs. One night she heard the bell and went downstairs, but no one was at the door, and everything was locked up.

In the same building, a fellow in a different area was quietly concentrating on a project. He was working in a storage space that contained old furniture. He was startled when an antique crib near him began rocking. He hadn't been moving, so he didn't brush against it, and there was no air movement to get it started.

Unseen Customers and the Extra Student

In another historic Cook Street building, in a street-level store that features craft materials, a guest artist was preparing to teach a class. While the artist, Maria*, was talking to the store's owner, the bell over the store's door rang repeatedly, but no one came in. Karen* who owns the store wasn't surprised. She told Maria that happens almost daily.

Maria went on about her business preparing for class. She didn't give another thought to the bell. Her students arrived and gathered in front of her at an oval table, and Marie started her class. While she was teaching, Marie felt there were four students, with three in her line of vision. Every time she turned to her right to include the fourth student, she'd be surprised to find empty space. While the students were busy, Maria joked to Karen about her invisible student. Karen understood. She said she often feels there's someone there with her, and at night the motion detector goes off four or five times. Maria wasn't fazed. She, like Karen, wasn't frightened by this unseen entity. As Maria left after class, she waved and said, "Goodnight, Madeline." That might not be the spirit's name, but Maria felt it was right.

Accounting Help?

Helen's* store is in a building built in 1886. After she closes for the day, she takes the money out of the cash register. Coins go in a little bag, and then she arranges the paper money so the portrait on each bill is face up and looking in the same direction. After that she locks the money in the safe. She's the only one who can open the safe. Once or twice a week, when she takes the money from the safe in the morning, she finds the bills have been rearranged.

Before closing the store, the store owner stacked the bills so they all faced the same way. In the morning, they were turned every which way. *Courtesy of Sharon Hart Addy.*

Comforting Company

Another Cook Street shopkeeper never feels lonely while she's at work. Although the occasional plop of something unbreakable hitting the floor might startle some, she's adjusted to the situation. At first it scared and annoyed her. Now, she considers it a sign that a friendly spirit is with her.

The things that fall aren't usually near the edge of a counter or shelf, and there's no physical reason for them to topple to the floor. On one occasion, the gentle plop came when she was very upset. She'd just learned that a dear relative had received a dreaded diagnosis. While she worked near a table displaying baseball-type caps, her thoughts strayed to her mom. She wished her mom was still alive to help the family through the difficult times ahead. When she heard the plop of something hitting the floor, she looked to see what fell and found a cap with the word "Mom" on it. The comfort of that word nearly brought tears as she hugged the cap and said, "Thank you" to the unknown spirit that keeps her company.

Basement Shenanigans

The businesses on Cook Street have seen a lot of changes over the years. A narrow bar in the middle of the business district reports shadowy figures and noises in the basement. It's said that some of the businesses had tunnels leading from one to the other. The tunnels could be a remnant of Prohibition days, when alcohol was forbidden by law and mobs ran liquor from place to place. If that's the case, the basement shadows could be bootleggers or rumrunners from the 1930s. Who knows?

Part IV
Apparitions in Repurposed Buildings

Organizations and businesses beyond Cook Street have also had unexplained events.

The Unhappy Member

Private clubs don't like to let people know they have unseen guests, but sometimes they do. Chris Okan and his brother created and ran SIGHT (Spirit Investigating Ghost Hunting Twins). Chris was working on his own when he was invited to a private club that asked him to investigate a presence felt in the upstairs closet where a distraught member hanged himself.

A K2 is a device that measures and records electrical output. The more output detected, the stronger the likelihood that you have a spirit in front of you. Chris explains the power by saying that if it's not a spirit setting off the K2's sound alarm, it's something that has the energy equivalent of a refrigerator. Chris set up his K2 and a recorder and left them in the closet. The K2 would detect the energy and set off the signal. The recorder would capture the signals. After three hours, he checked the K2 and recorder to see if there was activity. Nothing had been recorded, but the fresh batteries he'd put in the recorder were dead. The spirit drained them instead of setting off the K2. Chris felt a presence in the closet but had no evidence to back up what he knew was there.

MUSICAL PIPES

Quite a few of the large older homes in Portage were used in many different ways over the years. One of them, a lovely brick building on DeWitte Street, was a private residence. Then it became an official city building. Now, it's a museum.

Jerry* and a friend volunteered to help during renovations to the building. They were asked to paint a newly constructed wall on the first floor. He and his friend had regular day jobs, so they met in the evening to paint the wall. When they finished, Jerry gathered the paint brushes, said he'd clean them and told his friend he could go home. The basement had a large utility sink, so Jerry carried the brushes downstairs to clean them there. When he turned on the faucet, he heard tinny music coming out of the sink, as if it was from a record played on an old-time Victrola.

Having music come from a pipe seemed odd, but Jerry knew enough about how sound is carried to suspect that someone was playing music somewhere upstairs. He wondered if his friend had returned or someone else came to work in the building. He knew he was alone downstairs, so he went upstairs to see who was there. He checked both the first and second floor and didn't find anyone. Spooked, he left the brushes in the sink and went home. He'd come back another day—when he wasn't by himself—to clean them.

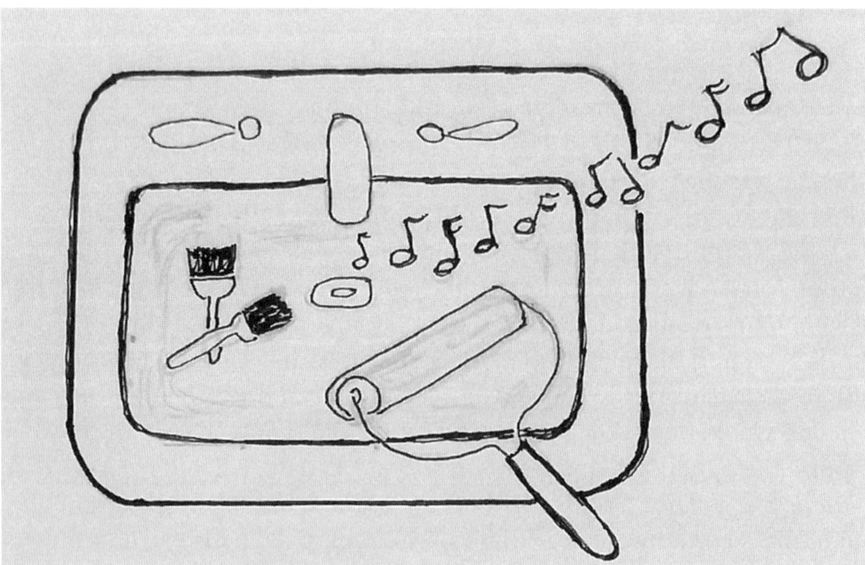

Jerry thought he was alone in the building, but there was music coming through the sink. What was going on? *Courtesy of Sharon Hart Addy.*

Get Out! Get Out!

In the early 2000s, Henry* rented the small apartment behind his restaurant to a middle-aged woman. She lived there happily for several years, so he was surprised when she called to complain about ghosts. She said she could see people walking through the walls and it was scaring her. Henry didn't completely believe this story but agreed to come over. He didn't know how to prepare for this kind of visit, but he'd purchased a large cross during a visit to Mexico. He brought it with him.

The night was dark and rainy, the kind of night when you can hear raindrops pinging off a car's roof. Henry loved the sound of rain. He decided to put his phone on the dash of the car to record the sound on the way over. He planned to play the recording later as a way to relax.

When he arrived at the apartment, he carried the cross through all the rooms, hoping it would scare the spirits. After about half an hour, the tenant said the spirits had stopped coming through the walls. At this point, Henry was a little concerned about the tenant's mental health and decided he would check on her more often.

By the time Henry got back to his car, the rain had stopped. He found his cellphone on the dash. He had forgotten it, and it was still recording. He decided to play back the recording as he drove home. The first few minutes he could hear the rain and the car running. Then he heard the car shut off, rustling noises and the door closing as he got out and went to the apartment. Rain sounds continued for a few minutes, and then he heard shouts of "Get out! Get out!" Apparently, the spirits were in a hurry to get away from him and his cross. The tenant never complained about spirits again.

The Restore

Can spirits remain in a building? The answer seems to be yes. The Restore is located on the south side of Portage in an enormous building that was once a grocery store. Now, the building is divided into two sections. The Restore is in one part, and a storage company occupies the other. When we—Shelley and Sharon—started researching paranormal activities in Portage, many residents told us the old Pick 'n Save is haunted. After hearing that comment so many times, we decided it was time to visit the Restore.

After a couple of calls and texts, we were able to connect with John Peruzzi, the director of development for Habitat for Humanity for the Wisconsin River Area. When we asked, "Did you know your building is haunted?" he said, "Oh yeah, we know." He told us he was aware of a lot of paranormal activity. We scheduled a time to come and investigate. We went during the day on a day the store was closed. We brought along a ghost meter pro and dowsing rods and planned to use a ghost box app.

A ghost meter pro measures electrical output and allows a spirit to communicate yes and no answers. Typically, we start by asking, "Are you a woman?" or "Are you a man?" After we have that basic information, we branch off to ask other things. Dowsing rods also connect with spirits. They allow the person holding them to ask questions that can be answered with yes or no. The rods swing open for yes and cross for no. The ghost box app is used through a smartphone. Spirit boxes have AM and FM radio receivers. A spirit sweeps through the stations, which sounds like white noise, and this will generate words. Sometimes the spirit provides whole sentences and at other times just single words. Here's what happened the day we visited:

> *On our investigation day we used our phones to film videos of the area. We captured a lot of orbs moving around the merchandise on the sales floor and in the back room where they sort through donated items. The most widely accepted orb definition is a light ball that is connected to a passed soul. You can usually see the orbs in a video, but sometimes they can also be seen with the naked eye. They come in different colors: black, white, green, red and blue. White is the most photographed and encountered orb. Orbs, when captured in a film, can either move very fast across the screen, jump, or meander.*
>
> *During our investigation at the Restore we also heard sounds: two poles tapping together, dressers being moved slightly. The ghost box captured the words "dwindle" and "blanket" on the sales floor. In the loading area out back, it produced the words "grass" and "limb."*
>
> *When we asked John if items fall or fly off the shelves, he said no. He did say he always feels there's a presence in the building—not a mean or aggressive one, just the feeling of someone being there. Occasionally employees complain that things are not where they are supposed to be, but that could be because customers sometimes move items.*

Restore was one of the few stores in Portage that let us report the building as having activity. We asked what made them decide to be named. John had

The Portage Restore sells gently used but well-loved furniture, building materials and fixtures. *Courtesy of John Lewis Peruzzi Jr.*

an interesting theory. Although the store carries a selection of new items, most of the things are donated. They were once the loved, prized possessions of someone, and that energy is connected to the item. When customers come in to shop, they're looking for something they can use and enjoy and perhaps even consider their prized possession. It's possible that the object's energy connects with the shopper. It's not a scary thing, just a cycle of life. Restore is a place to donate your things so someone else can make new memories with them.

Part V
Ghosts in Private Homes

Portage is filled with lovely homes. Many of them are over one hundred years old. Just looking at the buildings doesn't reveal their histories or hint at who lived there. Some of the buildings are still occupied by more folks than the eye can see.

The Angel in the Tree

Children are more open to the spirit world. They can often communicate with others behind the veil. Why is this? Perhaps life hasn't stepped in to stop this communication, or it could be that children are more open to the magic of our world. Whatever the reason, this next story tells of an interesting encounter.

Ellie* was an eight-year-old growing up in Portage. Her mom worked full time, sometimes until late in the afternoon. On those days, a friend of the family who had older children picked Ellie up and brought her to their house to play until Ellie's mom got home from work. The family friend lived next to a historic home in Portage. At the time of this story, the house next door was vacant. Ellie often played outside with the older children, who teased her that the house next door was haunted. Ellie wasn't quite sure what to believe until one fall afternoon.

The pounding stopped, and something flew out of the house and into the tree. *Illustration by Brett Kalwitter.*

The children were outside playing tag. The game had them running into the historic home's front yard. They heard a loud noise coming from inside the house that sounded like someone banging on the walls and windows. The children followed the noise to the back of the house. Something left the house and flew up to a nearby tree. Ellie described the entity as an angel. She said it reminded her of when you have a fire and above the fire you see shimmering heat. The angel looked like this shimmering heat but had the outline of a body with a head and wings. She could not make out a face.

All the children turned to each other, wondering if they all saw the same thing. As their fear grew, they did the natural thing when confronted with an unknown: they ran screaming to an adult. The mother listened to the story, but she didn't believe them.

Skepticism is a common reaction to such stories, as adults often attribute these strange occurrences to imagination. The fact that multiple children saw the same thing adds an intriguing twist. Ellie played at this house often over the years but never saw the angel again.

Kids in the Basement

In the summer of 2008, fifteen-year-old Jackie* was working for a friend's dad. Jackie and her friend were cleaning a house with two rental units. When both tenants moved out, Jackie and her friend came in to paint and prep the units for new renters.

After her friend left for the day, Jackie stayed. She wanted to finish painting the room she was working in. As she started to clean up her painting supplies, she heard three children playing downstairs in the basement. She knew they shouldn't be in the house. Jackie opened the door to the basement and could clearly hear the children moving around and laughing.

The basement had a dirt floor and was set up in the shape of a *U*. The middle was bricked up with a hallway leading around it. Jackie went downstairs. There was no one in the first section of the basement. She started down the hallway around the bricked-up section. She could hear the children up ahead, around the corner. She called out, saying they shouldn't be in the house. The children got quieter, but she could still hear them giggling. As she rounded the corner, she faced an empty space. A sense of cold surrounded her. She turned and ran upstairs, locked the basement behind her and left the building. She reported the incident to the landlord. He said he had heard tenants talk about that but didn't think much of it. Jackie never went back to finish painting.

Protector of the House

Guardian angels—we've all heard we have them, but few of us have met ours. Sue* knows she has someone watching over her.

Sue lives in a house built in 1875, while Portage was a growing community. Fort Winnebago had come and gone, but the railroad had arrived and the Portage canal had just been completed.

She and her husband moved into the old stone house in the 1970s. She liked living there so much that after they divorced she stayed there, but she started having experiences that led her to believe a spirit was in her home. The incidents have an interesting aspect: they only happen to women.

Many times over the years, during the night, Sue woke up to hear someone walk to the door of her bedroom and stop but not come in. Sue got the feeling that someone, perhaps a male spirit, is watching to make sure she's all right. Sue generally hears the footsteps around three or four o'clock in the morning.

During the summer of 2010, one of Sue's relatives, Jill*, was staying at the house while Sue was away on a trip. The young lady slept upstairs in one of two bedrooms located on the second floor. The first night of house sitting went well. On the second night around nine or ten o'clock, as Jill was settling down to sleep, she heard heavy footsteps come up the old wooden stairs and then stop at the top outside her door. Jill was terrified. She laid very still waiting for the door to open. After a few minutes, the footsteps went back down the stairs. She stayed where she was until she got up enough nerve to open her door. She stepped out of her room but didn't see anyone. Then she went downstairs to investigate. All the doors were still locked, and everything was in place. At first she thought she might be imagining things, but the mysterious footsteps continued the entire time she housesat. After getting scared the first night, she gradually accepted the presence and didn't let it bother her again.

A while later, one of Sue's daughters decided to move into the front bedroom, the one Jill had used at the top of the steps. Ginger*, a middle schooler, was old enough and responsible enough to stay by herself while her mom was at work. On the nights that her mom was working late, Ginger would go to bed around nine o'clock. Just as she was falling asleep, she would hear heavy footsteps climb to the top of the stairs and wait outside her open door. At first, thinking someone had come up the steps, she hid under the blankets, but the noise went away and she fell asleep. As the footsteps occurred more often, she stopped hiding. Instead she looked at the open doorway. She never saw anything or anyone there. On the nights when her mom was home, her mom would come upstairs to give her a hug and tuck her into bed. Ginger would lie awake after her mother left, waiting for the footsteps on the stairs. Eventually she realized she only heard them when her mother was gone. Sharing experiences led the family to believe that the unseen spirit comes upstairs to check on any girls or women who are alone in the house.

Who is this mysterious man who watches out for the women in the family? After searching the history of the house to see who'd lived there in the past, the family still doesn't have answers. For now the women's protector is still unknown.

THE BOY IN THE ATTIC

Have you ever wondered if the wonderful home you are buying still has ghostly tenants? Charlotte* often wondered this about her grandparents' home in Portage. In the summer of 2022, Charlotte was given the use of dowsing rods. In the paranormal community, dowsing rods help people connect with spirits. The person using the rods holds them so they point straight ahead. A spirit communicates by moving the rods open or closed to answer yes and no questions. Depending on the rods and the spirit, a yes could be open rods and a no could be crossed. The person holding the rods asks the spirit to show a yes and then a no. That's how the holder knows what the spirit answers.

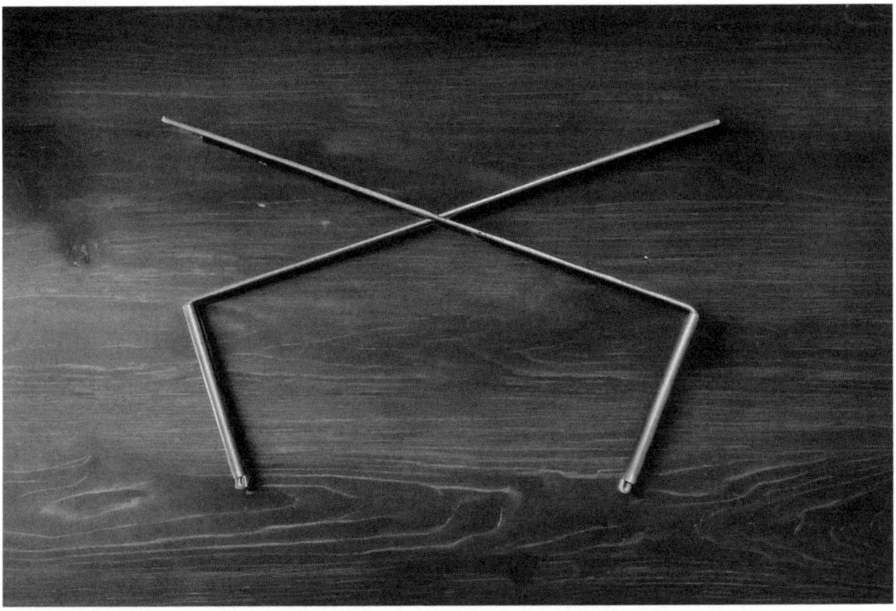

She took the dowsing rods around the house and asked yes and no questions. *Courtesy of Shelley Mordini.*

One day when she was visiting her grandparents, Charlotte decided to see if there were spirits in their home. She asked if there were spirits present. The rods immediately moved open to signify yes. She then asked if the spirit was a girl. The rods crossed, answering no. "Are you a boy?" The rods said yes. She asked, "Is your mom with you?" The rods moved to indicate no. "Is your brother or sister with you?" The rods moved to no again. "Is your dad with you?" The rods swung to say yes.

Charlotte took the rods around the house, asking, "What is your favorite room?" She asked, "Is the kitchen your favorite room?" No. "Is the living room your favorite room?" No. After many questions Charlotte determined that the spirits like to live in the remodeled attic, which currently is a bedroom.

Charlotte asked other questions. "Do you like me?" Yes. "Do you like my mom?" Yes. "Do you like Grandpa?" Yes. "Do you like Grandma?" No. No? Charlotte couldn't believe that! Everyone loved her grandma. The answer upset Charlotte so much that she didn't want to communicate with the boy anymore. She put the dowsing rods down and stopped talking to him, but she still wonders if he's around.

Little Things

When Laura* and her family moved into a house built in 1875, the previous owner warned them to expect some strange happenings. Now that they're settled in, they've noticed that, although the house may be old, it's not creaky the way some old houses are. However, when they're on the first floor they hear noises from the second floor. Footsteps. Crashes. If someone goes to investigate, they discover there's no one upstairs and nothing has fallen and hit the floor. Sometimes the ceiling fan and light turn themselves on and off. Laura's husband thinks it's the wiring or the switch, but Laura isn't convinced. At times their pets, both cats and dogs, turn to look as if something or someone is behind or beside them, but there's nothing there. Laura doesn't like the noises when they happen at night. Then they give her a fright, but she doesn't feel threatened, and the family has no plans to move.

Mourning Doves

Mourning doves are the most common birds in the United States. They're medium sized with small heads, slim bodies, thin necks and long tapering tails. Their wings have dark spots, and their heads and necks are pinkish-brown. They make a soft, drawn-out cooing sound like a lament, which gives them their name. Sometimes they're called rain doves or turtle doves. Although they're often seen perched on telephone wires, they're ground feeders that prefer seeds and willingly peck them off sidewalks and other areas. When they take to the air, they fly fast and straight. Many cultures see them as symbols of peace, hope, love or comfort.

Flocks of mourning doves and passenger pigeons were a common sight at one time. *Fred Galley Collection.*

This tale, which involves mourning doves, comes from the script of the Haunted Portage Wagon Tours that were available in the 1990s. The open-topped wagon would stop in the 300 block of West Franklin Street, and the guide shared this story with the passengers. A young couple bought a rundown house and discovered that mourning doves had taken over the attic and made a terrible mess. The man of the house spent weeks in the attic trying to clean it up. He developed a fatal lung disease from the bird droppings. In the years following his death, neighbors reported that they could, at times, still see him at the window clearing away the mess.

Cherry Tobacco

This is another story from the Haunted Portage Wagon Tour. A little farther down Franklin Street, the wagon slowed to a stop. Here the guide talked about Hugh Woodside, who loved to smoke a pipe filled with cherry tobacco. The story's setting is probably the 1930s, during the Great Depression. Jobs were scarce then, and men hopped aboard railroad boxcars for a free ride in the hope of getting to a place where they would find long-term employment.

The neighborhood, which was near the railroad tracks, was often visited by railroad bums who hopped off trains hoping to find a free meal or be hired to do some chore that would pay them something so they could get by for a while. When the railroad bums knocked on Hugh's back door, Hugh's wife, a soft-hearted woman, fed them. Hugh, concerned about safety, went out in the evening to patrol, making sure his property was safe and there were no peeping toms looking in windows or trying to break in and rob them. As he walked, he smoked his pipe. Now, years and years later, the evening breeze in this area sometimes carries the scent of cherry tobacco.

Checking In

Not all visitors are from the distant past. A recently widowed woman sat at her table one evening dealing with household paperwork. Something made her look up across the room to the chair where her husband usually sat. She saw him sitting there, smiling at her. Although he was transparent, she saw

The widow looked up and saw her husband smiling at her. Although he was transparent, she saw him clearly. *Illustration by Brett Kalwitter.*

him completely: his favorite faded jeans, his plaid shirt, his tousled hair, the gentle smile that wrinkled his cheeks, even the sparkle of mischief in his eyes. Delighted to see him, she asked how he was. Then, realizing he was dead, she laughed at herself, and he disappeared. But she did see him, so she knew he was still with her—as best he could be.

THE BONDS OF FRIENDSHIP

Joe* and Fred* were good friends all through high school. They played the same sports and loved the same foods. After graduation, they didn't go off to college; they stayed home and worked for one of the local factories. They had a tradition on Friday nights to meet for drinks and dinner. Joe fell in love with Sue*, and she joined their merry group. Not long after Joe found Sue, Fred met Lori*. The threesome became a foursome, and they kept up the tradition of Friday night drinks and dinner.

Fred decided to leave the factory job and found a job that required him to commute daily, thirty minutes each way. The drive wasn't bad, and typically he called Joe on his ride home so they could check in with each other.

One night in February, Sue got a call from Lori. It was Friday, and Sue was just getting dressed for dinner. Joe would be home soon for a quick change of clothes, and they'd be out of the house by five o'clock. Lori was hysterical. She had just gotten a call from the state patrol; Fred had died in a massive car pileup on the interstate. Fred was one of eight people who lost their lives in this accident.

Sue said that once Joe got home, they would head over to Lori's house. Sue had no idea how she'd tell her husband that his best friend was dead. She heard the front door open and Joe yell hello. Then he started talking to someone. Sue called to Joe, asking him to come into the bedroom. Joe came in and said, "Hey, Fred's sitting in the living room. How come you didn't get him a beer?"

Stunned, Sue asked, "Fred's in the living room?" Fred in her living room? Impossible.

"Yes," Joe insisted. "Fred's in the living room, but he didn't say much when I came in. I'll get changed and see what's going on."

Sue took Joe's hand and sat on the bed with him. "Joe, Fred died an hour ago on the interstate in a huge accident."

"You're crazy!" Joe shouted, jumping off the bed. "He's sitting in the living room." Joe started changing out of his work clothes. "Go see for yourself."

Bewildered, Sue went to the living room and found Fred sitting on the coach. The living room was freezing cold—as if the door to the wintry outside was open, but all the doors were closed. Sue approached the sofa. Fred looked up at her with a puzzled, sad look on his face. His lips were moving, but Sue couldn't hear anything. She was stunned. How could this be? Lori said Fred had died in an accident, but he was sitting right there.

Joe yelled from the bedroom, "Hey, Fred, I'll be right out. Let Sue know what you'd like to drink."

Sue couldn't take her eyes off Fred, and her teeth were starting to chatter from the intense cold. "Fred," she said, "you died an hour ago on the highway. I'm so very sorry." Sue started crying. Fred continued to look at her with the forlorn look. His lips were moving, but no sound was coming out.

Joe walked into the living room. "Geez, Sue, turn up the heat. It's freezing in here. Fred, what are you drinking tonight?" He headed for the kitchen to get drinks.

Sue said, "Joe, please come here."

Her tone stopped Joe. He turned around and stood in front of Fred on the sofa. "What's wrong with Fred? He doesn't look good."

"Fred died an hour ago on the interstate. Lori called. She's hysterical."

"That's impossible. He's sitting right here."

Just then Joe and Sue heard three loud bangs on their front door. Startled, they turned to look at the door. When they turned back, Fred was gone. Neither of them could believe what they had just seen and felt. It took hours for Sue to convince Joe that Fred had passed. Only after going to Fred and Lori's house and talking to Lori did Joe begin to believe that his best friend was gone.

Months later, Sue and Joe told Lori about the incident. Lori said, "Of course he would come and see you. You are his best friend in the whole world."

It seems not even the Grim Reaper can break the bonds of friendship.

PART VI
SENSITIVE ANIMALS

We often talk about people who are sensitive to spirits, but animals can be sensitive, too. The following stories are about cats and dogs and other animals, alive and dead, that interact with people and spirits in interesting ways.

It's said that pets that pass before their owners are waiting at the Rainbow Bridge. The following incidents might be examples of what pets do while they wait.

SWINGING TASSELS

Many of the buildings along Cook Street in downtown Portage date from the mid-1800s. Stores or offices fill the street-level spaces, with apartments or offices upstairs.

At 117 West Cook Street, Olivia Stefonek co-owns and operates The Mercantile, a store featuring the work of various artisans and vendors. She stayed late one night to catch up on things and was at work in her office in the back of the building. The store was closed and empty, the doors locked and the security cameras on.

A movement on the security camera's screen caught her attention. A closer look revealed the tassels and tags dangling from a display of scarves were moving. The scarves, hung on a low stand, almost reached the floor. She looked to make sure the door was closed. It was. There was no reason for a draft or any air movement in the area. As she watched the tags bobbing, she

Tassels and tags dangling from the display of scarves were moving, and Olivia saw the faint outline of a cat's paw. *Courtesy of Shelley Mordini.*

saw the faint outline of a cat pawing at the tags.

There are no records saying when the cat became attached to the building. The Wisconsin Historical Society has the building listed on the National and State Register of Historic Places. In 1884, the building housed a mill for grains. After 1915, it became a saloon as well as a flour and feed mill. According to the historical society's records, the building housed the saloon from 1894 to 1918. It was owned by Henry Epstein, who also operated a local brewery. Because transporting beer any distance was a problem, he opened the saloon to sell his brew. The ghost cat Olivia saw on her security camera's screen may come from that period. Back then it was a standard practice to have a "working cat" in the building to keep the rodent population in check. The building's owners supplied water and shelter, but other than that, the cat or cats had to fend for themselves. The building became a department store in 1937. It was called the Loid Atkinson's Federated Store. Since the building's days as a purveyor of general merchandise, it's gone through other changes. Today, it's The Mercantile.

The Dogs' Playmate

In the 200 block of West Cook Street, a general merchandise business with a large tailoring department opened in 1876. The basement was probably used as storage. Since then the building has had a succession of other successful businesses.

The current owner hired an accountant, who we will refer to as Joy*, and gave her an office space in the basement. She liked working on weekends and brought her two boxer dogs to keep her company in the empty building.

Sometimes the dogs turned as if someone had touched their backs. The interruptions were a welcome distraction. *Courtesy of Jill Addy.*

While she was working, the building was locked, and no customers or employees were present. On some occasions, her dogs ran up the stairs as if someone had entered the building and the dogs wanted to greet them. They'd look around at the top of the steps and then start back down. Sometimes as they came down the steps, they'd turn and look back, as if a ghostly hand had touched their backs.

The dogs' antics weren't a problem for Joy. The interruptions were a welcome source of exercise for the dogs, and she didn't mind the unseen visitors.

GEORGE, THE TIGGER-LIKE CAT

Sarah* loved her Maine Coon cat named George. George was a large cat, almost eighteen pounds, with long orange fur giving him the look of a lion. He was a great companion to Sarah, always meeting her at the door when she arrived home and sitting on her lap as she watched TV.

George had one strange habit. When Sarah went to bed and all the lights were off, he would jump off the bed and head down the steps to get a snack in the kitchen. It wasn't unusual that he wanted a snack; George *loved* to eat. What was unusual was the way he went down the stairs. It sounded as if he was hopping down the steps on two legs. Sarah said she envisioned him looking like Tigger and jumping down the stairs on his back legs. Sarah always giggled. In the morning when George went down the stairs with her, he walked down normally and didn't make his tromping noise, but his bedtime ramble sounded different.

Sarah and George enjoyed a long life together, but after eighteen years, George started to slow down. He developed cancer. At the end of his life, he weighed only four pounds. Sarah made the difficult decision to take him to the vet for a final visit. She said her goodbyes and left him there. Life would be strange without him, but she didn't want him to suffer anymore.

The first night Sarah went to bed without George, she rolled over and turned off the light. About a minute later, she heard George going down the steps with that unusual gait of his. She turned on the light, jumped out of bed and ran to the stairs. She didn't see anything on the steps. Sarah figured grief was making her hear things. She went back to her room and slept through the night. No other noises woke her up.

George thumped down the stairs like Tigger. *Courtesy of Suzane Colovski.*

The next night, Sarah went to bed, but she stayed up a little longer. Finally she turned off the light. Again, about a minute later, she heard something going down the steps, but this time Sarah was ready with a flashlight. She raced to the steps. No cat.

The nightly noise went on for weeks. It was only after Sarah went to bed and turned off her light that she heard the noise. She felt that George was still watching over her, a bond that not even death could break.

Eight weeks passed, and a coworker brought Sarah an orange tabby male kitten. He was little, with short hair and beautiful blue eyes. He wasn't George, but he was cute. Sarah named him Leo. On Leo's first night, Sarah brought his kennel up to the bedroom so he could be near her during the night. After she turned over to shut off the light, she waited in anticipation of the noise George made going down the steps, but nothing came. The next night, the same thing happened.

It seems that once Sarah wasn't alone, George could make the transition over the Rainbow Bridge.

No Dogs Outside After Dark

Sue* and John* rented an old farmhouse with many outbuildings. One of the outbuildings was a Quonset hut. The fields were rented to raise corn and soybeans. The property had been a dairy farm, but no cows were currently being milked on the farm. Sue and John owned a dog. Just before dusk, John liked to walk the dog down the path past the Quonset hut.

John heard voices in the Quonset hut. The dog began to growl, and all the hair stood up along his spine. *Illustration by Brett Kalwitter.*

On numerous occasions, John heard people talking in the hut but couldn't make out what they were saying. On the very first occasion he heard the voices, he shouted into the hut to ask, "Who's there?" The voices stopped. His dog began to growl, and all the hair stood up along his spine.

John led his dog back to the house, abandoning the walk. He told Sue what had happened. They left the dog in the house and went back to the Quonset hut to investigate. They both heard mumbling but were afraid to enter the hut. The couple, thinking of intruders, rushed back to the house to call the landlord. He came to investigate but found nothing. On other walks, John and his dog continued to hear voices from the Quonset hut but never saw a real person.

They lived on the farm for six months. Five out of seven nights, they would hear voices from the Quonset hut. They never stayed outside very long after dark. It didn't feel safe. If they got home after dark, they scurried into the house. Even the dog went out to pee quickly and rushed inside. The couple moved from the farm as soon as they could and vowed to never return.

Do Cats Have Nine Lives?

Do cats really have nine lives? When they die, do they go on to live forever?

A family moved to a house in the country and were enjoying their surroundings. Although not a new house, it met all their needs. The family brought their pets, a Siamese cat and a dog. The youngest girl talked to her mom about a scary encounter in the house. The daughter said she often met a cat on the stairs inside the house. What really frightened her was the feeling that a cat was walking on her bed while she was under the covers, but when she looked up, no cat was there. She told her mother, who asked if it was their pet Siamese cat. The girl said, "No. The cat was orange but slightly see-through." It was definitely not their cat.

Does a ghost cat catch ghost mice, or do they just play together? *Illustration by Brett Kalwitter.*

THE EERIE GREEN LIGHT

Farming has always been part of Columbia County. At first, pioneers grew everything they needed. By the 1870s and '80s, dairy farms dotted the area around Portage.

Sarah* and Josh* own a century farm in Columbia County. The farmhouse was built in 1880. It's made of fieldstone and is really just a cottage with two bedrooms and one bathroom, but it's ideally located near the barn and pastures. After the family built a larger house, they rented the cottage to Norman*, their hired man.

One evening in mid-November 1992, Norman was returning from town after some grocery shopping. It was about eight o'clock on a dark, rainy evening. Norman pulled up to the cottage and started to unload his groceries, but something made him look around. The barn door was slightly open. An eerie green light spread from the barn out into the barnyard.

An eerie green light radiated from the open barn doors, and Norman found the cow traumatized. *Courtesy of Kyle Martin.*

A cow had given birth that day and was in the pen closest to the door. Norman wondered if Josh had put a heat lamp near the calf. But since the weather wasn't very cold, he wondered why Josh would do that—and why it was a green light and not a normal red one.

Norman carried his groceries into the cottage and went to investigate. As he walked toward the barn, he heard a high-pitched whirring sound. The closer he got to the barn, the louder the sound became. The intensity of the sound grew until Norman had to bend over and cover his ears. While he was bent over, something whooshed over his head, lifting his hair. When he stood up and looked at the barn, the green light was gone. So was the sound, but the forty head of cattle and ten pigs inside were making a lot of noise. The milking cows were stomping their feet and mooing in their stanchions. In the pen nearest the door, the new mother cow was guarding her calf. Norman wanted to make sure the calf was all right, but the mother cow wouldn't let him anywhere near it. The closer he got, the more she charged at him, a very unusual behavior for a Holstein cow. He was finally able to see the calf was okay, just shivering. He dug out a heat lamp and put it over the pen, then he fed all the animals to settle them down. It was close to ten o'clock before the animals quieted, more than an hour since he noticed the green light spilling out of the barn. Whatever caused the light and that unbearable noise really upset them.

Norman is still perplexed by this situation. He's never had it repeated, but to this day, he can't figure out what spooked the animals. Where did the green light come from, where did it go and will it come back?

Part VII
Country Ghosts

When Europeans arrived, the area that became Portage was a mix of forest and grasslands with some low, swampy areas as well as highlands overlooking them and, of course, the Fox and Wisconsin Rivers. The wetlands provided an excellent habitat for tamarack trees. Tamaracks are an unusual member of the pine family. They grow in the wet soil of swamps and bogs. Their needle-shaped leaves turn yellow in fall and are shed. Tamaracks are sometimes called the eastern or American larch. Because they grow in wet, boggy soil, they're somewhat water resistant and are used for poles and posts. The wood is tough and durable. The trees grow tall and straight, which made them an excellent building material in the days of early Portage.

North of Portage, pine forests became the source of lumber used for corduroy and plank roads, log cabins and traditional buildings. New Pinery Road led lumberjacks to large stands of trees that would be harvested during the winter. In spring, the logs were sent down the Wisconsin River in rafts to become lumber for the homesteads and towns popping up in the area.

The Portage area is dotted with farms. At first they were subsistence farms, growing the crops and animals families needed to sustain life on the frontier. One such group of farms in Newport Township northwest of Portage was known as the Moe Settlement. Norwegian families established homesteads and built a church, which became the center of all community gatherings. A town—with stores and services—never developed, but the farms and the church remain. Other farming communities spawned towns as entrepreneurs recognized the need for a general store, blacksmith, wagonmaker, hotel and so on.

While towns grew and changed, so did farming. In the late 1800s and early 1900s, W.D. Hoard and the University of Wisconsin encouraged farmers to become part of the dairy industry. The magazine *Hoard's Dairyman* became a source of information and education. It played a big role in turning Wisconsin into the Dairy State. Today, corporate dairy farms have replaced many of the family-owned dairy farms, but many small cheese companies are still in business.

The city of Portage is surrounded by smaller communities, many of which have roots as farming centers. These include Pardeeville and Briggsville to the northeast and Cambria, east of Pardeeville. The township of Lewiston is northwest, with Caledonia to the southwest.

Pardeeville, which is near the headwaters of the Fox River, was named for John S. Pardee, a businessman from Milwaukee who built a store in the area in 1848. One of its most famous residents was Theresa West Elmendorf, who became the first female president of the American Library Association. She served as president from 1880 to 1890. She married librarian Henry Elmdorf in 1891 and, being a married woman, had to give up her job.

Times have changed since single women had only slightly more freedom than married women. In the past, a single woman might have had to live with family. Today, that's not the case. Single women can, and do, rent apartments.

All the Clocks Stop at 2:22 a.m.

Lois* needed a place to live. She went to see an apartment in the upper level of an older Victorian house in the city of Pardeeville. The apartment felt warm and inviting, so Lois signed the lease. On the first night Lois spent in the apartment, all her clocks stopped at 2:22 a.m. She thought this was weird, but she assumed the batteries were bad and put new ones into all her clocks. The second night in the apartment, all the clocks stopped at 2:22 a.m. again. Lois replaced the batteries again. By the third night of the clocks stopping at 2:22 a.m., Lois knew she had unseen company. She felt it was the spirit of an older woman. She didn't feel threatened in any way, but she was curious. She did a bit of internet research and learned that 222 is

Night after night, all the clocks in Lois's apartment stopped at 2:22 a.m. *Courtesy of Sharon Hart Addy.*

the number associated with balance, collaboration, love and harmony. Lois guessed that by stopping the clocks at 222, the spirit was letting her know she was welcome. Lois was glad to be accepted; she just wished the spirit would leave her clocks alone.

The Woman at the Window

Shirley's* mother moved to a new house outside Briggsville, north of Portage. Shirley's mom was very happy to be in her new home, but she noticed the empty house across the street. No curtains hung in the windows, and no one visited the building. It seemed unoccupied.

One day Shirley visited her mom and looked across the street at the empty house. She saw a middle-aged woman with brown hair pushing a curtain aside to look out at the street. Shirley could see her only from the waist up. Shirley blinked and looked again. There were no curtains and no one in the window. The woman Shirley saw looking out the window from the vacant house across the street might be a residual haunting.

Have you heard the term "residual haunting"? A residual haunting, according to the Travel Channel paranormal glossary, is paranormal activity resulting from the energy imprint of a person or event in time. This could be a place memory or a residual loop of smells, sounds and noise. Residual energy is emotional energy that can be imprinted by a living or crossed-over person. It can attach to clothes, furniture, objects and places. These strong emotions stay with the item or site and sometimes reappear as loops. An example is the spirit that walks through the building once a month or hearing sounds of a party in an empty building.

In her book *Ghosts Among Us*, Leslie Rule recounts the experience of Sadie Rouss and her husband, Philip. While driving from Atlanta, Georgia, on Highway 78 toward Memphis, Tennessee, they encountered travelers who were out of place next to this two-lane highway: a wagon train that looked like it was straight out of a western film. The first wagon had an elderly couple sitting up front. The man held the reins and had a pipe clenched in his teeth. The woman was wearing a white bonnet. The Rousses were astonished by the sight. After they had traveled two blocks, Philip looked at his wife and said, "We need to meet those folks." He turned their car around to find the wagon train, but it was gone. They pulled over on the side of the road where they first spotted the wagons and found nothing to indicate a wagon train had gone through. Although the grass was wet and the ground spongy, there were no ruts to show wagon wheels had rolled across the ground recently.

THE HOMESTEAD

An old homestead sits west of Portage near the Baraboo River. It's on a rise overlooking a natural spring of clear water. Native Americans camped in this area, as documented by the many arrowheads found in the river flats in front of the house. The farmhouse and older barns were built in 1869.

Annie* and her husband, Jim*, moved to this farm in 1987. Annie was pregnant when the couple moved in with their two-year-old. They began raising horses. Over the years, Annie has had unusual experiences in the house and around the property.

After living on the land for a number of years, Anne consulted a psychic. The psychic told Annie that a Native American couple was connected with an old barn on the back of the property, near the spring, and they were pleased to see the land used as a horse farm.

Some of Annie's experiences are visual. At times, from the corner of her eye, Annie sees a lady in the house wearing a long, dark dress. When Annie turns to look at her, no one is there. In 2010, Annie was doing chores in a new barn down the hill from the house. She watched her daughter's car as it left the yard and headed toward town. She looked across the road and saw

Annie looked across the road and saw a tall, thin man. He walked rapidly up the hill and disappeared. *Illustration by Brett Kalwitter.*

a tall, thin man wearing a farmer's hat. He walked rapidly up the hill and disappeared. She went to see where he went, but he'd vanished.

Sometimes Annie hears things she can't account for. One night at about eleven o'clock, while Jim was at work, Annie heard heavy footsteps in the hallway coming toward the bedroom. They sounded like a man's heavy boots. The clomping stopped just outside her bedroom door. This happened only once. Periodically, Annie hears voices. Sometimes they say "Whatcha doin'?" or "Hey Annie." These greetings are infrequent and separated by months or years. Once while working in the barn, Annie heard voices coming from outside. She listened for a while, puzzled. It sounded like a crowd had gathered in front of the barn doors. She stepped outside and found the barnyard empty and silent. The psychic whom Annie consulted walked through the buildings and grounds and explained that the crowd noise was residual energy from a farm auction.

In 2018, while walking up from the barn, Annie heard words and mumbling and caught a vision of an older, gray-haired, disheveled man in a canvas army coat. He walked with her for about twenty feet and disappeared. The psychic Annie contacted said the man lived there during the 1930s, when the government outlawed alcohol. The man had been a bootlegger. His wife kept him sober, but after she died, he and his son went back to making whiskey. They used their wonderful spring water and corn mash to make their moonshine.

Before she left, the psychic told Annie that the antique mirror she bought at a secondhand shop acted as a portal through which spirits came and went. The psychic blessed and smudged the house with sage. That seemed to calm the spirits down.

Noises in the Country

Keith Bylewski has an unusual profession. He's a ghost hunter and has been since 1978. His company is called Wisconsin Investigating Paranormal. Keith's team typically includes a woman, because women are more sensitive, and a minister. Keith and the minister work in tandem to deal with spiritual problems and unfriendly entities.

Over the years, he's encountered numerous spirits in the Portage area. One intriguing story takes place in rural Portage at an old farmhouse. The team was called in to help clear out a spirit.

The group arrived at the old farmhouse in several vehicles and parked in the driveway. One of their trucks' horns started blaring. Nothing they tried would stop the noise. They moved the truck to another location, and the horn was quiet. A team member arrived late and parked where the truck had been. A few minutes later, her car horn began to sound constantly. She moved her car, and the noise stopped.

This particular house had a couple of interesting problems. The rocking chair in the upstairs bedroom sometimes rocked as if someone was soothing a baby. There were reports of a crying baby that could not be comforted.

The people who lived there also reported orbs and cold spots. Keith speculated that the house had so many problems because many of the antiques had spirits connected with them.

The empty rocking chair moved back and forth as if someone was soothing a baby. *Courtesy of Sharon Hart Addy.*

Keith used flashlights to communicate with the spirits. Paranormal investigators use two flashlights of different colors. Keith's flashlights are black and red. He unscrews the tops of his flashlights to break the contact between the battery and bulb. With that contact broken, the only way the flashlight can produce a beam of light is if a spirit controls it. The flashlights are placed on a flat surface. Keith explains to the spirits that one of the flashlights should be used to signal yes and the other to signal no. Although the bulb is disconnected from the battery, spirits can provide enough energy to turn on the flashlights and make them flash. Typically, the investigator announces the black flashlight is for "no" answers and the red flashlight is for "yes."

While investigating the upstairs bedroom, Keith put his hand on the rocking chair; it felt very cold. Keith had a spirit box with him. A spirit box is a white noise machine that allows the spirit to say words through the box. The frequency of the white noise is used to generate speech. While using the spirit box upstairs, Keith asked the spirit who was rocking in the chair, "Where did you go?" He got the answer "Up." Then he heard voices and a baby crying. Keith wondered if the mother had passed or the baby. He had no answers to these questions.

During the investigation, Keith also used a spectrum camera. Full-spectrum cameras allow you to see the full spectrum of light, including infrared and ultraviolet frequencies. The camera works like a regular camera, but it captures pictures of phenomena such as orbs or shadows. Keith's photos captured pictures of spirits with the wall as background.

With permission of the property owner, an exorcism was performed by the minister. The family has not had any unusual experiences since then.

BALLS OF LIGHT

Chris Okan of SIGHT (Spirit Investigating Ghost Hunting Twins) and his brother visited an old farmhouse in Pardeeville. While they were there, orbs appeared and then disappeared and reappeared in another place. These orbs were seen with the naked eye and in pictures and videos taken with a digital phone.

You can catch orbs in a picture; however, if you take your phone and select video, the orbs and their movements are easier to observe. Orbs generally appear as white balls of light. According to the Merriam-Webster dictionary, orbs are the residual energy of celestial bodies moving around a space.

The orbs Chris saw zoomed through rooms, floating and fluttering. The family who lived there had called Chris because the orbs frightened them. Chris's investigation helped the family understand this paranormal activity was not demonic and they would never be harmed; they were simply residual hauntings. The family accepted Chris's explanation and, over time, were able to ignore the orbs.

ECHOES FROM THE PAST

Sue* and John* always wanted to live in the country. When a house became available just outside Portage on a road leading toward Cambria, they jumped at the chance and moved in. Then strange things began to happen.

John came home for lunch at 11:30 a.m. one day. It was a nice day, so he left the back door open with the screen door in place. He began to make his lunch when he heard the front doorbell ring. He stopped preparing lunch and went to answer the door. No one was there. He walked through the house and went out the back door, thinking the visitor was walking around the house. He reached the front yard without seeing anyone. He scratched his head and went inside to finish his lunch. About five minutes later, he heard "Hellooo" coming from the front of the house. The voice sounded like an older female. He rushed to the living room and checked the front door. No one was there.

When Sue and John talked to their landlord about this strange event, the landlord said it was interesting. He explained that his aunt had passed away in the house. In fact, the house was originally hers, and he had inherited it only the year before.

Sue and John jumped at the chance to live on the old farm but didn't expect an invisible caller. *Fred Galley Collection.*

And there were other odd events. One day, Larry*, a friend of the owner, came to cut grass around the outbuildings. He stopped John and asked if he had felt or heard anything unusual on this property. Rather hesitantly, John said he sometimes heard voices in one of the outbuildings. Larry said he'd never go near that building. It felt unfriendly and not safe, so much so that he worried about being attacked when he was near the building. Larry also pointed to the many black walnut trees near the back of the building. No matter how many times he trimmed the branches, he would always get a branch in the face as he was mowing, usually when he least expected it. He also only mowed the lawn during broad daylight. If it was getting toward dusk, he cleaned up as fast as he could and got out of there before the sun set. John followed his example and avoided that building and didn't venture out after dark.

THE ICEHOUSE STORY

Before refrigerators were invented, ice was harvested from lakes and ponds during the winter, put in storage and sold to homeowners and businesses to keep things cool during the summer. The blocks of ice were stored in icehouses, which were usually located partly or completely underground and often built near a natural source of ice like a river, pond or freshwater lake. The ice blocks were stacked and insulated against melting with straw or sawdust. They would stay frozen for many months, sometimes even until the following winter. Icehouses have been in use for centuries. Cuneiform tablets dating from 1780 BC record the construction of an icehouse in the northern Mesopotamian town of Terqa. In the United Kingdom, the use of icehouses continued until the 1960s.

In Portage, brickmakers' clay pits, like the one that became the pond at Pauquette Park, were important sources of ice. Workers waited until the ice was several feet deep and then, using saws, cut the ice into blocks. Huge tongs helped workers lift the blocks to sleighs, wagons, trucks or whatever was used to haul them to an icehouse. The blocks were delivered to homes and stored in an icebox, an insulated cabinet usually made of wood. Iceboxes had two compartments. The block of ice went in one, with a drip pan under it. The other compartment was for food that needed to be kept cold. Ice picks, which resemble a huge needle with a handle on the end where the eye would be, were used to break off chunks of ice. The chunks were put in glasses and pitchers or just enjoyed as a cold treat on a hot summer day. Iceboxes were probably used in Portage until the 1930s, when electric refrigerators became available. The next story takes place near the location of an old icehouse.

In 1993, the Jones* family decided to build their dream house on a hill near Swan Lake. Neighborhood gossip said the area was once a Native American burial ground. The land had been undisturbed for many years, but a developer bought the section and started to put up houses. The lot the Jones family purchased included the foundation of an old icehouse. The family decided not to disturb the icehouse and built farther away from this structure.

The problems started almost immediately. When the basement was dug, it was three feet too deep and had to be redone. The roof joists were taller than needed for the home and needed to be reordered. It seemed like everything had to be done twice. When the family finally moved into the house, odd things happened with the lights. Family members would turn off a light when leaving a room, only to return moments later and find the light on.

Many people report such experiences, which might be linked to various factors, including environmental conditions, electrical issues or even psychological factors. Some people look for logical explanations, but others interpret these experiences as potential paranormal activity. Was there some energy in the house from the icehouse era? Some paranormal enthusiasts believe that certain locations retain residual energy from past events or emotional imprints. Could this be an example of that?

For the Jones family, having a light come on after it's shut off might possibly have been an electrical problem, but the house was new. There were also other odd events. In the middle of the night, family members would wake up to the sound of a conversation taking place in the house. They'd walk through the house only to find everyone else asleep. Some family members woke up at 3:11 a.m. several times during the week. In consulting the book *Angel's Numbers* by Doreen Virtue, 311 means change is coming. Was the clock's time a warning from a spirit? After living in the house for almost three years, a member of the family developed a serious health condition, and they decided to move. No one was sad about leaving.

"Please Don't Scare Me" and the Transparent Man

Helen* was never comfortable in her house. When she came home, she opened the door and chanted, "Please don't scare me. Please don't scare me."

Her chant didn't mean she was afraid of spirits; she just didn't want to be frightened by them. She really wanted to see her mother and her grandmother again, even as spirits. She especially wanted to see her mother, whose death had been tragic. Helen was still struggling to come to peace with it, but she was terrified when she thought about seeing a ghost. She often said, "Please don't scare me," over and over when she was alone.

Helen went to see a psychic hoping to connect with her mother and grandmother. The first thing the psychic told Helen was that there were two women who wanted to speak to her, but they wanted her permission. They didn't want to scare her. Helen found the session with the psychic a very healing experience, and it brought her peace.

The psychic also told Helen that her daughter had the ability to see spirits. The daughter had never said anything to her mother about that ability, but the psychic insisted it was true. After the visit, Helen asked her daughter Stacy* about her ability, and Stacy shared her experience with the guest room.

Stacy said she'd walked past their guest room and saw the back of a man wearing a suit sitting at the desk. Shortly after that, Helen's husband was ill, so Helen moved to the guest room. One night after dark, while lying in bed, she felt someone sit on the foot of the bed. When she looked there, the space was empty and the door was still shut. After that, Helen refused to sleep in the guest room. It was too creepy.

Stacy discovered their unseen resident must have been a businessman. She was sitting in the living room one day when she looked up and saw a man walk through the room. She described the fellow as colorless—black and white and see-through—wearing a suit and carrying a briefcase. The man did a little nod and wave, opened a transparent door where the original front door had been and left. Stacy never saw him again.

The Side-Gabled Log House Investigation

The owners of an estate outside Portage called Shad Thurston and asked if his organization, Wisconsin Investigating the Paranormal, could look into the strange things happening on their property. The odd events centered on two buildings: an old side-gabled log cabin and a lighthouse-shaped building.

The two-story log cabin was built between 1870 and 1880. It was a traditional cabin made of logs stacked horizontally to form the walls. The roof sloped down over the front and back, forming a triangular shape on the ends. The design became popular because it works well. The slanted roof allows for an attic or a loft for extra living space. The slant also sheds rain and snow. The tall sides on the cabin's ends and the lengthy front and back provided plenty of space for windows at a time when natural light was necessary.

The building Thurston was called in to investigate was very fancy for the 1880s. The kitchen had clapboard walls covering the logs. Clapboard walls consist of long, thin vertical boards that fit together with a clapping sound. They overlap, creating a solid protective surface. The owners of the property used their log cabin as a guest house. Many of their visitors reported paranormal activity. Eventually no one wanted to stay in the log cabin, which led them to contact Thurston and his paranormal team. They wanted to find out if the stories were true.

When the team arrived at the guest house, they found a thick fog covering the floor, but in places the fog was parted as if someone had just walked through it. The fog didn't move as the investigators stepped into it, and it remained there, motionless, while they investigated. No other paranormal activity was discovered at the log cabin.

Fog covered the log cabin's floor and parted as if someone had walked through it. *Courtesy of Sharon Hart Addy.*

Thurston and his team moved on to the two-story house shaped like a lighthouse. No one was living in the building at that time, but many people saw an older woman who might be in her mid-seventies rocking in a rocking chair near a second-floor window. She wore clothing from the Victorian era, and her hair was pulled back into a bun. The owners had no record of someone matching that description associated with the building.

Thurston found evidence that confirmed what the owner's guests had been saying.

THE WHISTLER

When Disney's animated version of *Snow White and the Seven Dwarfs* hit movie screens in 1937, the song "Whistle While You Work" became a big hit. The idea of whistling while you work is an old one. Folklore says that slave owners made kitchen slaves whistle so they couldn't eat the food they were preparing. Although few people whistle these days, most folks, like Snow White and the dwarfs, find music helps them as they go about their daily tasks. Music, they say, makes the burden lighter. Before radio and other devices, whistling was a way to create your own music to work by.

Sarah* and John* weren't whistlers, but someone on their farm was. The farm dates from 1905. The barn was the first building built on the property. The upper level has a large haymow, with thirty stanchions and four pens in the lower area. Sarah and John bought the property in the 1970s and turned it into a dairy farm.

Almost immediately they started having strange experiences in the haymow. When they were working alone in the upper area of the barn, they would hear whistling. They'd hear the same couple of bars repeated for about a minute. Neither Sarah nor John recognized the tune, but the feeling that came with it was friendly. Sarah and John got in the habit of saying, "Hey, Joe" to greet the unseen worker. They called him Joe because Joe seemed like a good name for him. After about a year, the couple knew the tune quite well, but they still didn't know what it was called or if there were words to it. They decided to ask family members if they had ever heard it. When John whistled the tune, his grandpa's eyes grew wide. He said he had heard it often when he was on a naval ship during World War II. He explained that if you worked in the engine room of the ship, sailors whistled it to keep on track and beat back boredom.

Curious, Sarah and John researched the previous owners of the property. None of them served in the navy. One former owner remembered a hired hand who liked to whistle, but he wasn't sure if the fellow had been in the navy. When John whistled the tune, the fellow shouted, "That's it! That's the tune he whistled!" John asked for the fellow's name. The previous owner sheepishly put his head down and explained, "We just called all the hired hands Joe because they changed so often.

Perhaps that's why greeting the unseen whistler with "Hey, Joe" seemed so natural.

Part VIII
Tales from Cemeteries

Native American Burial Grounds

Native Americans created low effigy mounds to mark an area they traveled or lived near. Some of them contained human remains and therefore are considered burial mounds. The mounds have many different shapes. Some are linear, like a wide dash with rounded ends; conical, like a small cone-shaped hill; or molded into the shape of an animal or a human being. The mounds were found singly or in groups, usually along waterways or cut banks along rivers. A cut bank is also called a river cliff or an outside bank.

Man Mound north of Highway 33 between Portage and Baraboo is a well-maintained effigy mound. More easily accessible mounds are part of a wayside about ten miles west of Portage on Highway 16. Called the Kingsley Bend Mound Group of Columbia County, the site contains over twenty mounds in a parklike setting. This group of mounds is unique because they typically contain a single burial per mound.

Effigy mounds were found across southern and central Wisconsin and also in Minnesota, Iowa and Illinois. Some mounds stand alone, while others are in groups. A survey conducted in the 1940s for the State Historical Society of Wisconsin by Charles Brown reported 274 mounds in Columbia County. About 26 of those mound groups were in or near the city of Portage. Because they rose only a foot or two above the ground, many mounds

The Kingsley Bend Mound Group is an interesting stop along Highway 16 between Portage and the Dells. *Courtesy of Shelley Mordini.*

weren't recognized as something other than the natural rise and fall of the land and were destroyed as the city grew or farm fields were plowed.

Within the city of Portage, the historical society's records list four prehistoric sites. A few contained Native American remains. The August 8, 1904 issue of the *Portage Daily Register* referred to the 300 block of East Conant Avenue as "an Indian cemetery" approximately two or three city lots in size. The discovery was made while excavating for a new building. Along with human remains, a calumet and silver bracelets were found. Other Native American burials were unearthed in the area of East Cook Street between Adams and Jefferson.

JOHN LECUYER'S GRAVE

The area we know as Columbia County was still Native American land when the first entrepreneurs came to make sure furs and other trade goods crossed from the Fox to the Wisconsin River without mishap. John Lecuyer was among that vanguard.

Information about his final resting place was found in *Tales of Old Portage*, a book of newspaper columns written by Dorothy McCarthy for the *Portage Daily Register* from 1958 to 1975. The columns were compiled into a book published by the Portage Historical Society. In McCarthy's article "What's Become of John Lecuyer's Grave?" she quoted A.J. Turner, a historian and the editor of the *Portage Daily Register*. Here's a brief version of why the early pioneer has a rather unusual burial site and memorial.

John Lecuyer, who was also known as John L'Ecuyer, came to the wilderness in 1798. At that time, Laurent Barth had a trading post on the Wisconsin River as well as a successful business moving goods both ways across the portage between the Fox and Wisconsin Rivers. Lecuyer purchased the Fox River side of Barth's transportation business. Barth continued to handle passengers, furs, food and whiskey moving east from the shore of the Wisconsin River.

When Lecuyer died in 1810, there were no set cemeteries, so his remains were buried at the top of the hill north of the portage. The white picket fence surrounding his grave became a local landmark. His grave was so well known that in 1832 it became the northern point of a roughly triangular land claim referred to as the Grigon Tract or French Claim No. 21.

Over time the reason for the fence must have been forgotten. The city grew, and Lecuyer's gravesite was lost—until 1904 or 1905. Government surveyors working to establish the limits of the Grigon Tract ran the lines of the claim. They located the northern point in front of a home's bay window. A small excavation revealed Lecuyer's bones about two feet below the surface. The remains were left as they were and immediately covered. A short time later, a flower bed appeared on the spot—a sweet tribute to an early settler.

Pauquette's Lost and Found Remains

Pierre Pauquette came to Portage around 1818. He'd been hired by John Jacob Astor to establish a trading post for the American Fur Company on the Fox River.

Pauquette, a fair-minded, gentle giant, became a well-respected member of the growing community. Along with running Astor's trading post and overseeing shipments from one river to the other, he also ran a ferry service across the Wisconsin River. Because he was fluent in English, French and Ho Chunk, he was often an interpreter during Ho Chunk dealings with the U.S. government.

The first Catholic church in the Portage area was also the first final resting place of Pierre Pauquette. *Fred Galley Collection.*

During the early days, before Portage grew to the size of a city, East Cook Street between Adams and Jefferson was known as the Old Catholic Cemetery or Cook Street Burial Grounds. This area was also the first final resting place of Pierre Pauquette.

After Pauquette was shot and killed during a dispute on October 10, 1836, he was buried under the church he helped build near Adams and Conant Streets. A fire destroyed the log building in 1840, but trees surrounding the church marked Pauquette's final resting place. By 1852, not quite twenty years after his death, officials decided the growing town needed a regular grid of connecting roads. One of those roads, Adams Street, cut through the vacant land where the church once stood. During road construction, Pauquette's coffin was found. Friends reburied him nearby, but they didn't mark the spot. For the next fifty years, Pauquette's grave remained unmarked and eventually forgotten. On August 19, 1904, workers digging a building's foundation unearthed a badly decaying wooden coffin. A metal name plate identified the six-foot skeleton as Pierre Pauquette. His remains were moved to the Catholic cemetery on the north side of town, where they were placed with other members of his extended family. They have not been moved since.

Dead Man's Crossing

Seven miles west of Portage, in Lewiston Section 26, a man took his life near the railroad tracks that run alongside Highway 16. When he died, Portage was a village, Highway 16 didn't exist and the railroad ran through a wooded pasture. He was found by ten-year-old Augusta Martin, who was herding the family's cows home to her parents' farm. Augusta saw the man leaning against a tree and thought he was sleeping. When he was still there in the morning, she told her dad.

Rumor said the man was one of the "Knights of the Road" who fell off the train. But evidence suggested something else. William Blank, a railroad foreman at the time, said the man lived south of Portage in the town of Pacific. An empty box of Paris Green, an arsenic-based organic pigment, was found beside him. Those who found him surmised he'd swallowed the Paris Green to forget the trouble he was having with his wife. No one claimed the body, so the railroad section crew put together a rough coffin and buried him where he died. Volunteers from the railroad planted oak

The final resting spot of a "Knight of the Road." *Courtesy of Shelley Mordini.*

saplings at the head and foot of the grave to mark it. Years later, other volunteers surrounded the burial site with a white fence. Gus Oeftger, who heard the story from Blank, said the trees were about six inches around when he started working for the railroad in 1902. Volunteers still maintain the fence around the grave. The area is known as Dead Man's Crossing, and the man's identity is still unknown.

BURIED ALIVE

In 1884, if you showed no signs of breathing or a heartbeat couldn't be detected, you were pronounced dead and buried within days. Fear of disease was one reason bodies were promptly committed to graves; another, probably more important, is that bodies that are not embalmed decompose quickly. Embalming had been in use since the Civil War (1861–64), but it wasn't always available in rural areas.

Sarah A. Smith of Pardeeville, Wisconsin, was a young woman married to Anderson Smith. Sarah was thirty-one years old and had teenage children at home when she was declared dead on March 27, 1884. Thirteen years later, Sarah's coffin needed to be moved to another location in the cemetery, so it was exhumed. When it was opened, viewers found her body partly turned, her right hand drawn up to her face and her fingers bitten through. In an article reporting the findings, the *Wisconsin State Journal* stated that the fingers being bitten off is typical of a person finding themselves buried alive. Apparently, she'd been buried while in a trance or coma.

Efforts to prevent this from happening included an aboveground bell that the person in the coffin could ring and air passages to allow the person to breathe and call for help. None of that had been available for Sarah.

ST. MICHAEL'S LUTHERAN CEMETERY

St. Michael's Lutheran Cemetery is located on Church Road between Wisconsin Dells and Portage in Lewiston Township. It's surrounded by private property. The cemetery is closed from dusk to dawn, and police will ticket anyone loitering on the road at night. Occasionally, special permission to visit the cemetery is granted by Lewiston Township.

The St. Michael's Lutheran congregation erected their first church in 1859 about six miles from Portage, just off Highway O. This vibrant church and congregation was called the Mother Church of St. John's Lutheran Church–Missouri Synod in West Wisconsin. In 1927, the church building was sold and moved to Dekorra, Wisconsin. The cemetery remained in place.

The churchyard contains about sixty graves and no longer allows burials. The public is asked to be respectful. Many of the people who live in Lewiston Township have loved ones buried in this cemetery.

Local legend suggests that a girl hanged herself near the entrance to the cemetery, and her apparition can be seen at times hanging from a tree. There are reports of visions, disconnected voices and a feeling that overwhelms a person's senses.

On one occasion, Keith Bylewski and his paranormal team were granted permission to be on the property at night. They heard a lot of noises, but they couldn't identify their origin. They also captured orbs and visions in pictures. One of the most interesting pictures was of a woman with her hair in a bun but no visible body. Another picture captured a man's head, but again, he had no body.

CRYING IN THE CEMETERY

Crystal* has always been interested in spirits. During the winter of 2020, when her friends suggested a late-night visit to St. Michael's Cemetery, she was up for the adventure. The group arrived at the cemetery, left their cars and gathered to talk. They intended to wander around the area and wanted to have a plan in case someone got lost. While they were talking, they heard a young girl crying in the cemetery. They spent about twenty minutes looking for the little girl before the crying stopped as suddenly and mysteriously as it began.

The group stayed together and wandered around the cemetery. They saw a bright glowing orb appear behind a tombstone. As they approached, the light went out and the orb suddenly disappeared. After that, Crystal went home. She'd had enough adventure for one night.

Photo Fright

During the fall of 2011, Sally* decided to drive out to the old Church Road Cemetery. She was just getting into photography and loved taking macabre pictures. She went to the cemetery to photograph the different trinkets people left on the graves. The items intrigued her. She was careful to not photograph names or dates out of respect for those buried there. She left at dusk and then went to hang out at a friend's house. She got home about ten o'clock. As usual, she turned off her phone, plugged it into an outlet in the kitchen and went to bed.

Just after five o'clock the next morning, her sister Anna* burst into her room crying and screaming, "That isn't funny! Stop doing that!" Sally finally got her sister to calm down and tell her what was going on. Anna's phone rang at five o'clock. The call came from Sally but not really from Sally—from Sally's phone. Anna listened as the voice on the other end kept whispering, "What are you doing? What are you doing?" Phone records show the call was a minute and a half long.

Sally felt like she had somehow insulted the spirits at the cemetery and they were on her phone. She immediately deleted the photos and drove out to the cemetery to apologize. After that, she never returned to the cemetery, and there were no more calls made by spirits from her phone.

Visitors to the Church Road Cemetery

Shad Thurston's organization, Wisconsin Investigating the Paranormal, has been around for a while. The team looks into different types of unexplained phenomena. They've had some interesting and potentially paranormal experiences at St. Michael's Cemetery.

Investigating paranormal phenomena is a unique field that often involves a combination of technology, personal experiences and a willingness to explore and experience the unknown. The use of touch lights and maglights as tools to communicate with potential spirits is a common practice in paranormal investigations. Many believe that spirits may be able to manipulate electrical devices or energy to communicate with the living.

During one of Thurston's team's nocturnal visits to the cemetery, their maglights turned on and off three times by themselves and then stayed off.

Ghostly children played tag among the headstones. *Illustration by Brett Kalwitter.*

Moments later a car full of teenagers arrived. It seemed as if the spirits were using the maglights to let the team know they were about to get company.

Disembodied voices and sightings of ghostly children playing tag at the cemetery are also common reports in paranormal investigations. These experiences are often difficult to explain through conventional means, leading investigators to consider supernatural or ghostly explanations.

It's noteworthy that the team had permission to investigate at Church Road Cemetery. Accessing private property without authorization can lead to legal issues. It's always important for paranormal investigators to respect property rights and obtain permission before conducting investigations.

Part IX
Murder, Myths and Lore

Some stories continue to be passed along even when there's little or no evidence to support them. Many of the tales in this section couldn't be verified. Others are well documented.

The Woman with the Baby Carriage

Several books about hauntings in Portage report a lady dressed in 1900s-style clothing pushing an old-fashioned baby carriage down West Franklin Street to where it meets West Wisconsin Street. When someone approaches her, she vanishes. Some accounts say she's seen around 9:00 p.m. Chad Lewis and Terry Fisk, authors of *Wisconsin Road Guide to Haunted Locations*, traveled this part of the road from 8:30 p.m. to 9:30 p.m. but didn't see the woman. This story is widely reported by members of the Portage community, but many of those repeating the story haven't seen her personally.

Mob Rule

The intersection of Wisconsin, Cook and Witt Streets once formed a pentagon in the heart of downtown Portage. In occult tradition, that ancient shape symbolizes power and protection. Perhaps it does, perhaps it

In the past, several highways met in front of the Raulf Hotel, creating a pentagon. *Fred Galley Collection.*

doesn't. In 1869, William Spain was arrested for murder and thrown in the Portage jail. A mob, angry and determined, stormed the jail. They pulled Spain from his cell and hanged him in the pentagon, across from what is now the Raulf Hotel. The mob, still enraged and seeking justice, returned to the jail, grabbed a rapist and hanged him too. Today, the pentagon is gone, as Witt Street ends half a block away from the intersection. Perhaps traffic tangles led to the change, but then again, there may have been other reasons.

STATES RIGHTS

This could be considered a bit of mayhem, or maybe it was just plain love. Chauncy Roberts bred horses and had a lively interest in politics. In the 1850s and '60s, the question of states' rights was a hot political topic in the United States. Roberts firmly believed that states should have more power than the federal government. To support his belief, he named his favorite pacer States Rights. The bay stallion was fast for his time. He was reported to run the mile in two minutes and twenty seconds. On July 9, 1889, Roberts entered the twenty-eight-year-old horse in a race. States Rights ran until his

Chauncy Roberts loved his favorite horse and named him States Rights. *Courtesy of Shelley Mordini.*

heart gave out, and he died during the race. Roberts hated seeing his beloved horse lying down.

He took States Rights home and had him buried standing up. Roberts erected a monument over the grave in the tiny triangular plot where the Fort Winnebago Town Road runs into the Old Military Road, about five miles east of Portage. The memorial is still there today.

A WAYLAID HONOR

The city of Poynette, which is south of Portage, was to be named in honor of Pierre Pauquette, the early settler who worked for John Jacob Astor's American Fur Trading Company. Pauquette ran a trading post on the Fox River and supervised the transportation of furs and other goods across the portage between the Fox and Wisconsin Rivers. He also ran a ferry business across the Wisconsin River and acted as an official interpreter in government dealings with Native Americans. His contributions to the early days of European activity in the area led James Doty, governor of the Wisconsin Territory to lay out a village and name it Pauquette. However, during the process of applying to set up a post office for the settlement, the name was misspelled, changing Pauquette to Poynette. Attempts to rectify the clerical error were unsuccessful, and the town's name remained Poynette.

THE DUEL

This story comes to us from the Haunted Portage Tour developed in the 1980s by The Portage Chamber of Commerce. Carol Lavine was one of the tour guides. According to legend, two men who owned property near the intersection of Dunn and West Franklin Streets had an argument. One of them even called for a duel with pistols. Apparently, the duel never took place. Some say that if you listen carefully, you can still hear the two men arguing.

Shootin' the Ghost

This story from *Spooky Wisconsin*, written by S.E. Schlosser, brings haunting to a new level. Details in the author's version of the story, which supposedly took place in the Portage area, indicate it comes from the era before farms had electric lights.

One night while a farm family was eating supper, they heard footsteps overhead. Their first thought was that a burglar was upstairs. Fear of fire from a dropped candle or smashed lantern was their next thought. The dad grabbed his rifle, and he and the eldest son tiptoed up the steps. When they reached the top, the sound stopped. They searched the dark bedrooms and didn't find anyone. After they rejoined the rest of the family at the dinner table, the footsteps sounded again. The dad, rifle in hand, and son went back up the steps with the same result. The footsteps stopped when they reached the top of the steps, and they didn't find anyone in any of the rooms.

After a sleepless night, the family went through the whole house. No one was hiding in a wardrobe, under a bed or in the attic. That night at supper, the footsteps came again, pacing back and forth upstairs. The dad grabbed his gun and charged up the stairs. The footsteps stopped when he reached the second floor. His sons, carrying lanterns, followed him as they searched. They didn't find anybody.

For the next week, the man and his sons raced up the steps each time they heard the pacing during dinner. Finally, they accepted the fact that they had a ghost and speculated as to where it came from. The general consensus was that the ghost moved to the house after the barn burned. Each member of the family had a different idea of who the ghost might be. The father thought it might be a soldier who died of wounds in 1882 during the Blackhawk War. The oldest son guessed it might be a trapper or hunter who died before Wisconsin became a territory. The wife suggested it might be a Jesuit priest, anguished by the way Native Americans were treated while settlers poured into Wisconsin seeking land.

Not long after that conversation, the ghost started playing with the broom that was kept in the summer kitchen, a building separate from the house. During hot weather, meals were prepared there and vegetables from the garden were canned there. Cooking in the summer kitchen kept the house cooler. One day the mother went out to the summer kitchen to get the broom and couldn't find it. The family looked everywhere and finally found it under the oldest son's bed. The mom took a lot of teasing and

The broom was moved so many times that the family finally chained it to the wall. *Illustration by Brett Kalwitter.*

put the broom back in the summer kitchen, but the next morning it wasn't there. Every day all summer long, the family had to search for the broom. They found it in the cellar, in the horse barn, in the cornfield, under a bureau and even in an apple tree in the orchard. The dad tried chaining it to the summer kitchen's wall, but in the morning he found the chain in pieces and the broom on the back lawn. The family gave up. They'd just have to live with the ghost or ghosts.

Summer eased into fall, and hunting season came. The dad and neighbor took their guns and spent the day in the woods and fields near the farm. After they came in, the family invited the neighbor to stay for supper. When the footsteps started overhead, the family just ignored them, but the neighbor was surprised. He thought the family had another guest who hadn't been asked to come down for supper. The homeowner and his wife didn't know what to say. They were embarrassed to admit the house was haunted, but the kids weren't.

The neighbor got up and said, "Well, it's time we did something about that!" He grabbed his shotgun and headed for the stairs. The wife asked what he intended to do, and the neighbor said, "I'll scare it away." The wife scolded him, saying that she didn't want him shooting his gun in her house. He insisted the gun wasn't loaded.

The neighbor tiptoed up the stairs. He jumped to the upstairs hallway with a loud scream and pulled the trigger on the gun. The gun went off with a huge blast that sent wallpaper and plaster flying. The family ran upstairs to find out what had happened. They found the neighbor feeling foolish and a hole in their wall. The oldest son asked, "Did you hear that moan? I think he shot the ghost."

Shaking their heads at the silly idea, they all trooped downstairs. The neighbor apologized over and over and was forgiven. At least he'd done something. They all settled down to finish their meal, listening for the overhead footsteps to start again. In the silence, they heard whimpering coming from the root cellar under the house. The oldest son took a lantern and opened the trapdoor to the root cellar. Everyone crowded around as he stepped onto the ladder. When he reached the ladder's second rung, the sound stopped. His search of the cellar didn't find anything unusual, but after that day they never heard footsteps on the second floor, and the broom stayed put.

THE BRIDAL POND

Heavy September fog and road construction were responsible for the untimely death of a young couple in this true story. Portage's Zona Gale, who won the Pulitzer Prize for drama in 1921, used this tragic story as the basis for her novel *Bridal Pond*. Gale, a Portage native, earned her bachelor's and master's degrees in literature at the University of Wisconsin–Madison. After working for newspapers in Milwaukee, Madison and New York, she came back to Portage, and her hometown became source material for her novels. Hers were among the first novels to reflect the everyday life, customs and concerns of small-town residents.

Zona Gale's writing changed fiction. She was the first to use the drama of small-town life in stories and plays. *Fred Galley Collection.*

Gale's work includes short stories, essays, poetry, magazine articles and movie scripts as well as her books. *Bridal Pond* was published in 1943, years after the actual event. Here's an account of what happened.

Twenty-two-year-old Hazel Ferguson grew up an only child on a dairy farm near Marshall, Wisconsin. Her home was without indoor plumbing or electricity, which was common for country houses at the time. The house itself was beautiful with wood floors, sliding panels (pocket doors), nine-foot ceilings and two porches. She was happy at home until she fell in love with outgoing, friendly Johnny Pirkl. Her parents didn't approve of the match because Johnny was Catholic. When Hazel refused to give him up, her parents told her they wouldn't attend the wedding. Hazel, determined to marry the man she loved, moved to her future in-laws' house and lived with them in the weeks leading up to the ceremony.

Johnny Pirkl, part of a large family, bought a house near his family's farms on September 7, 1927, for them to move into after the wedding. The home cost $8,307 and was a modest two-bedroom structure with slanted floors. The wood stove in the kitchen was the only source of heat for the building. The payments on the five-year mortgage were sizable, but the future bridegroom was optimistic in his happiness.

Before the wedding, Johnny took his sister Alta and her young daughter Dorothy shopping in Madison. His niece was to be the flower girl at the wedding, and he wanted her to have a special outfit. They picked out a dress and a fancy headpiece with rhinestones and two doves. Alta was alarmed at the price, but Johnny insisted he wanted his niece to be beautiful for the wedding.

Although the early fall colors in Marshall had been gorgeous, the weather was dull and dreary on the wedding day, Tuesday, September 27. Marrying on a weekday was a common practice at that time. Hazel wore a lovely gown and a veil for the 9:00 a.m. Latin Mass. She carried a bouquet of large roses. After the service, in their delight, Hazel and Johnny signed their marriage certificate on the wrong lines. To amend the mistake, someone crossed out "bride" and "groom" and added the correct words next to their names. Johnny listed his occupation as farmer, and Hazel listed "at home."

With the ceremony over, the happy couple left the church in a hail of rice thrown by their friends. Wedding photos were taken, and then the wedding party and about twenty-five guests gathered at Johnny's parents' house a few blocks from the church. A huge table with eight-foot-wide inserts stretched from the kitchen into the dining room to accommodate everyone. After the meal, there was music. Johnny's sister played the piano while the guests sang, the maid of honor played songs on her twelve-string ukulele and a phonograph provided popular tunes. Just before four o'clock, Hazel changed into traveling clothes and pinned her corsage on her coat. Johnny, in his wedding suit, still wore his boutonniere in his buttonhole.

At the car, Johnny's new 1927 Chevrolet coach, they found a "Just Married" sign on the trunk and old shoes and tin cans tied to the bumper. They were eager to be on their way in spite of the fog rolling in. Johnny's mother pleaded with the newlyweds to stay overnight and leave for their honeymoon in the morning, but they refused. She cried as she waved goodbye. Perhaps her tears were prompted by a psychic reading she'd had as a young woman. She'd been told, long before she married and had children, that one of her children would die young.

The very next day, Johnny's sister Alta saw Sorenson's hearse pass their house heading west. Alta's daughter Dorothy, the little flower girl, remembered her mother crying and saying that she'd had a premonition that something had happened to Johnny.

Newspapers reported that the couple was last seen at 6:45 p.m. in Portage, where they stopped and asked for directions to Baraboo. They headed west on Highway 33. The dirt road was full of potholes with only a few houses along it. Rumor has it that county crews working on the road took down the signs and reflectors directing traffic around the curve that takes vehicles past Pauquette Park and to the bridge over the Wisconsin River. The fog was thicker near the river. Johnny missed the turn, drove between two trees and splashed into the Pauquette Park pond. The pond—originally a quarry providing clay for the bricks used in Fort Winnebago and houses in town—was deep.

In the morning, puzzled state highway employees followed tire tracks from the road to the pond. There they discovered a car submerged in seven feet of water. They initially thought the car was abandoned, but they found Johnny and Hazel inside it. The windshield was broken, and the bride and groom both had skull fractures. There were no signs of struggle or attempts to get out of the car. Johnny's hands clutched the steering wheel, and Hazel sat beside him, her arm across his shoulders. The bodies were taken from the

Fog hid the pond in Pauquette Park, making it the scene of a tragic accident. *Courtesy of Shelley Mordini.*

car and the car towed from the pond. Besides the windshield and water, the car's only other damage was a dent in the back left side.

As was customary at the time, Johnny and Hazel were taken to Johnny's parents' house, where they were laid out. The flowers that had decorated the house for their wedding reception became their funeral flowers. Hazel was in her wedding dress and veil with her bouquet of roses in her hands. Johnny wore his wedding suit. The church where they'd had their wedding on Tuesday became the site of their funeral on Saturday. They were laid to rest in a double grave.

To prevent further accidents of this kind, a low rock wall with an entry arch was erected near the curve. It was shortened when Highway 33 was widened, but it's still there, hopefully preventing future tragedies.

Where the North Begins

Traveling by car became popular in the 1920s. People eager to escape to the clear air and beautiful scenery of northern Wisconsin traveled one of the many highways that cross in Portage. Tourists frequently stopped in Portage for meals and lodging.

To support the growing tourist industry, the newly organized Portage Chamber of Commerce created a campground and a wayside offering travelers' necessities in Riverside Park along Highway 33 on the south side of town. They also adopted the slogan "Where the North Begins" and posted the wording on the shelter they had erected there. The shelter and the sign are there to this day. Portage continues to be "Where the North Begins."

Pierre Pauquette's Hidden Gold

A local legend says that in the early 1800s, Pierre Pauquette buried seventeen kegs of gold on his property on the west shore of the Wisconsin River.

Pauquette was an early resident of the Portage area. He was born near St. Louis but learned the fur trade—trapping and trading—while living with Native Americans in the West. He arrived in what was to be the city of Portage about 1818 to manage John Jacob Astor's fur trading post on the shores of the Fox River, not far from where the Indian Agency House would be built. Astor, who controlled his fur trading empire from Prairie du Chien, sent Pauquette to make sure shipments of furs crossed the short stretch of land dividing the Fox and Wisconsin Rivers safely and honestly. Some of those offering to transport goods between the rivers inflated their prices.

Pauquette, who was well over six feet tall, had unbelievable strength. He was able to lift an eight-hundred-pound cask of white lead off the ground, and there's the tale that when an ox failed while pulling a wagon across the portage, Pauquette took its place. His mental prowess was also admirable. He never learned to read or write, but he spoke French, English and Ho Chunk and was able to keep track of accounts in his head. He was mild mannered, good-natured, friendly, generous, moral and trustworthy. His abilities brought him to the attention of the United States government. Pauquette became a vital link between the Ho Chunk and government representatives.

At one point, he was commissioned to teach the Ho Chunk the basics of farming. With eight yokes of oxen and some farm utensils, he set up what became known as the Indian Farms on the western shore of the Wisconsin River. He built a home there in 1833 and began a ferry service taking people and goods across the river. He continued to handle the trading post on the Fox, as well as acting as an interpreter and go-between for the U.S. government and the Ho Chunk nation.

For the 1800s, he was probably considered a wealthy man. With no banks to keep funds safe, money and valuables were buried. In September 1968, his house was still standing, but it would be demolished to make way for the new Highway 33 bridge to be built across the Wisconsin River. Because of the legend of Pauquette's gold, there was the possibility that fortune hunters might dig up the area and undermine the bridge. To keep that from happening, personnel from the Wisconsin Highway Department scoured the area with metal detectors and bulldozers. Technical equipment and assistance were provided by the Department of Natural Resources and the State Crime Laboratory. Representatives of the Community Arts staff of the University of Wisconsin and the attorney general's office were also present. In spite of the extensive search and all the experts who helped, nothing was found.

Was the gold there and someone had already found it, or was the story just a bit of lore? We might never know.

The Old Nursing Home

An abandoned, rather contemporary-looking building on the west side of Portage is said to be haunted. What was once the Divine Savior Nursing Home has architectural elements reminiscent of buildings by Frank Lloyd Wright. Henry R. Slaby of Milwaukee was the project's architect. In the 1960s, he designed many Catholic churches, hospitals and monasteries, including the Mother of Good Counsel Church and the Sacred Heart Monastery, which has a unique round chapel; both of these are Milwaukee-area landmarks. He oversaw the planning and construction of the Divine Savior Nursing Home in 1966.

The facility operated for about thirty years, closing in the 1990s. Around 2010, the building was sold to a developer who wanted to turn it into a retirement home for veterans. Unfortunately, he passed away before he could see his dream come true.

Neighbors and those walking past the abandoned nursing home sometimes see lights, even though the building has no power. *Courtesy of Shelley Mordini.*

The building stands empty. Some of the windows are broken, and "No Trespassing" signs are posted around it. People who walk past say they sometimes see someone gazing out a window, but when they look back, there's no one there. Although the power has been turned off, people say they sometimes see lights inside. In the years since the building was actively inhabited, it has fallen into disrepair, and its future is uncertain. Some say the building should be torn down. If the building is haunted and it's demolished, where will the ghosts go?

THE LOST COINS

From rural Portage comes a story of intrigue that spans many generations. Sam* lived on his family's farm just a stone's throw from downtown Portage. He was a gentleman of German descent who worked hard all his life farming his land. One day Sam received a letter telling him that he'd inherited a large sum of money from a relative. He was overjoyed. He didn't believe in banks, so he cashed the check he'd received, changed the bills into coins, put them into small jars and buried them on his property. Sam continued to live his life according to his frugal bachelor ways. He never spent the money he'd inherited. Sam passed away in his eighties, and

Sam took the money, turned it into coins and hid them around the farm. *Courtesy of Gordon Addy.*

his nieces and nephews came to clear out the house and outbuildings and put the property up for sale. The family boxed up his papers and clothes to sort through at a later time.

About a year after the property was sold, one of his nieces was going through Sam's papers and found a rudimentary map detailing the location of the money jars. She shared the news with her family, and they came up with a plan. They approached the owner of the property to ask if they could look for the lost money and said they'd split the amount they found with him. The owner declined the offer. He then proceeded to dig all around the farm but didn't find anything. Recently Sam's family made an offer to purchase the farm. As of the writing of this book, nothing has been confirmed. Maybe someday we'll hear more about the lost coins of Columbia County.

BIBLIOGRAPHY

Animal and Dairy Sciences, University of Wisconsin–Madison. "History." andysci.wisc.edu/about-us/department-history.

Aptowicz, Cristin O'Keefe. "Surgery in a Time Before Anesthesia." Live Science, September 25, 2014. www.livescience.com/48003-anesthesia-was-once-devils-work.html.

Austin, H. Russell. *The Wisconsin Story.* Fourth printing, Journal Company, 1958.

Brownstown Historical Society. "The Old Corduroy Road." www.brownstownhistory.org/announcements/the-old-corduroy-road.

City of Portage Church Hill Historic District. www.portagewi.gov.

Cole, H.E. *Stagecoach and Tavern Days in the Baraboo Region.* Sauk County Publishing Company, 1923.

Curtis, Ina. *Early Days at the Fox-Wisconsin Portage.* Times Publishing Company, 1974.

Derleth, August. *The Wisconsin: River of Thousand Isles.* University of Wisconsin Press, 1985.

Forestry. "Tamarack Tree." forestry.com/trees/tamarack-tree/#google_vignette.

Fort Winnebago Surgeons Quarters. fortwinnebagosurgeonsquarters.org/surgeonsquarters.html.

Fradkin, Philip L. *Stagecoach Wells Fargo and the American West.* Thorndike Press, 2002.

Friends of the Office of State Archaeology. "Corduroy Roads." www.fosa-ct.org.

Goc, Michael J. *Land & Lumber: A History of Portage County.* Portage Historical Society and New Past Press, 1999.

———. *Portage: A Sesquicentennial History*. Portage Historical Society and New Past Press, 2004.

Habitat for Humanity. "Habitat's History." www.habitat.org/about/history.

Hamilton, John. *Haunted Places*. ABDO Publishing Company, 1996.

Historic Portage, WI, Downtown & Waterfront Walking Tour. Brochure, 2016.

Isaacs, Sally Senzell. *Stagecoaches and Railroads.* Kingfisher, 2012.

Jacobson, Ryan. *Ghostly Tales of Wisconsin.* Adventure Publications, 2009.

Kinzie, Juliette M. *Wau-Bun: The Early Days in the Northwest.* National Society of the Colonial Dames of America in the State of Wisconsin Old Indian Agency House, 1989.

Kleist, Frederica Hart. *Fox-Wisconsin "Portage" 1673–1987 Portage, Wisconsin.* F.H. Kleist, 1987.

———. *Portage Heritage at Fort Winnebago Area.* F.H. Kleist, 1984.

Krulos, Tea. *Wisconsin Legends & Lore*. The History Press, 2020.

LaVigne, Carol. Script for Ghostly Legends on Society Hill tour given in Partage in the 1980s. Not published, tour no longer given. Script used with permission of the Portage Chamber of Commerce.

Lesy, Michael. *Wisconsin Death Trip.* Anchor Books, 1991.

Levi, Hannah Heidi, and Brian G. Borton. *Famous Wisconsin Ghosts and Ghost Hunters*. Badger Books, 2005.

Lewis, Chad, and Terry Fisk. *The Wisconsin Road Guide to Haunted Locations.* Unexplained Research Publishing Company, 2004.

Longfellow, Rickie. "Plank Roads." U.S. Department of Transportation. highways.dot.gov/highway-history/general-highway-history/back-time/plank-roads.

McCarthy, Dorothy. *Tales of Old Portage: Articles Written by Dorothy McCarthy as They Appeared in the Portage Daily Register.* Portage Historical Society, 2010.

McGann, Dennis. *The Wisconsin Story.* Milwaukee Journal, 1957.

McKay, Joyce, principal investigator. *An Intensive Historical Architectural and Historical Survey of the City of Portage, Columbia County, Wisconsin.* Portage Area Chamber of Commerce. Kathy Taylor, project director. Brookhaven Press, 2006.

Nehring, Craig, and Melissa Clevenger. *Wisconsin Haunted Travel Guide*. Self-published, 2022.

Olson, Gerald. *Opening the High Prairie of Southwest Wisconsin: A New Vision: The Roles of Inns and Stages, circa 1838 to 1918.* Self-published, 2016.

Paquette, Moses. "The Wisconsin Winnebagoes." hotcakencyclopedia.com/ho.Pauquette-WisconsinWinnebagoes.html.

Poynette, Scott De Laruelle. "Pierre Pauquette: Myth and Man." HNG News, April 3, 2013. www.hngnews.com/poynette_press/news/local/yesterday---pierre-pauquette-myth-and-man/article_c8ff7724-9c66-11e2-b73b-001a4bcf6878.html.

Rule, Leslie. *Ghosts Among Us*. Andrew McNeel, 2004.

Russell, John M. *Wiscomical.* Johnson Litho Graphics of Eau Claire, 2003.

Russell, Lou, and John Russell. *Wisconsin Lore and Legends.* Oak Point Press, 1982.

———. *Wisconsin Lore and Legends.* Vol. 2. Oak Point Press, 1983.

Schlosser, S.E. *Spooky Wisconsin.* Globe Pequot Press, 2008.

Soil Survey of Columbia County. Bulletin 49. Madison, Wisconsin, 1916

Tekiela, Stan. *Trees of Wisconsin Field Guide*. Adventure Publications, 2002.

Todd, Lewis Paul, and Merle Curti. *Rise of the American Nation.* 2nd ed. Harcourt, Brace & World, 1969.

Travel Wisconsin. "Fox-Wisconsin Portage Site." www.travelwisconsin.com/museums-history/fox-wisconsin-portage-site-203902.

Tully, Richard M. *A Man Called Baraboo.* Ballindalloch Press, 2007.

Uhl, Cassie. "Understanding Residual Energy vs. Spirit." www.cassieuhl.com.

U.S. Department of Veterans Affairs. "Fort Winnebago Cemetery Soldiers' Lot." www.cem.va.gov/cems/lots/Fort_Winnebago.asp.

Varnum Continentals. "Quonset Hut History." varnumcontinentals.org.

Virtue, Doreen. *Angel Numbers 101: The Meaning of 111, 123, 444 and Other Number Sequences.* Hay House, 2008.

Whitlock, Jennifer. "The historical Timeline of surgery." Verywell Health, April 15, 2024. www.verywellhealth.com/the-history-of-surgery-timeline-3157332#.

Wikipedia. "Agoston Haraszthy." en.wikipedia.org/wiki/Aroston_Haraszthy.

Wisconsin Historical Society. "Early History of Fort Winnebago." www.wisconsinhistory.org.

———. "Early U.S. Settlement: Military Outposts in Wisconsin." www.wisconsinhistory.org/Records/Article/CS395.

———. "Letters About White Incursions onto Indian Lands in 1827." content.wisconsinhistory.org/digital/collection/tp/id/59891.

———. "Logging: The Industry That Changed the State." www.wisconsinhistory.org/Records/Article/CS409.

———. "Roads in Wisconsin (Early)." https://www.wisconsinhistory.org/Records/Article/CS1825.

———. "The Surrender and Captivity of Ho-Chunk Warrior Red Bird." www.wisconsinhistory.org/records/article/CS294.

Wisconsin 101. "Object History: Plank Roads." wi101.wisc.edu/object-history-plank-roads.

Wood magazine. "Western Larch." www.woodmagazine.com/materials-guide/lumber/wood-species-3/western-larch.

YouTube. Faces of the Forgotten. "Her Fingers Bitten to the Bone—Sarah Smith Buried Alive in 1884." youtu.be/DKhMB4Es0-s?feature=shared.

About the Authors

Courtesy of Purple Lotus Studios.

Shelley Mordini is something of a juggler. She's a retired high school special education teacher and the owner of Baraboo Tours. During the summer, Shelley offers historic and haunted walking tours of Baraboo. Her historic tours give you a chance to follow in the footsteps of the Ringling Brothers and see the legacy they left behind. The haunted tours present a unique aspect of the area around the Square in the heart of downtown Baraboo. Her blue rickshaw is a familiar sight during the Thursday night Concerts on the Square as she takes her passengers on a quick ride. Shelley is an avid traveler. Not content to just visit spots around the world, she's expanded her tour business into a full-service travel agency. On the local level, she's involved in civic activities, serving on committees and holding offices as she works to improve her hometown. Her love of Baraboo is apparent in her book *Haunted Baraboo*, which, like *Haunted Portage*, combines history with the astral activities that fascinate her. Because of her outgoing nature and the many activities she's juggled over the years, she knows a great many people, but she's always glad to meet more. If you have a ghost story, she'd love to hear it. Contact her at baraboortours@yahoo.com.

Courtesy of Jill Addy.

Cricket, *Ladybug*, *Highlights*, *High Five* and other magazines for children have published Sharon Hart Addy's stories, poems, articles, word puzzles and crafts. She's happiest when she gets up in the morning, turns on her computer and has lots of time to write. Christmas and Halloween are her favorite holidays. Thanksgiving is wonderful because her family is all together, but it means cooking, which isn't her greatest talent. She'd much rather be stirring characters into action than mixing mushroom soup and green beans into a casserole. Sharon is the author of several picture books, including *Lucky Jake*, *When Wishes Were Horses* and *Right Here on This Spot.* She was honored to be asked by the Adams County Historical Society (Wisconsin) to write a book memorializing Katherine McGowan, a well-known local educator. Interviews with those who knew Katherine and research in the historical society's archives and the public library resulted in *K: A Girl's Life in Friendship, 1905–'06.* Her work for adults has appeared in several magazines and the anthologies *Heartbreaks & Half-Truths* and *Moonlight & Misadventure*, published by Superior Shores Press, and Holiday Hijinks' *Whimsical Winter Wonderland.* She likes to mix history and humor and make fun of her no-talent cooking in the blog she occasionally posts at sharonaddy.wordpress.com.